MYTHS AND MONSTERS

FROM DRAGONS TO WEREWOLVES

MYTHS AND MONSTERS

FROM DRAGONS TO WEREWOLVES

By
Laura Buller

Consultant
Philip Wilkinson

A Dorling Kindersley Book

Dorling **DK** Kindersley

LONDON, NEW YORK, MUNICH,
MELBOURNE, and DELHI

Project Editor Emma Johnson
Project Art Editor James Marks
Senior Editor Fran Jones
Senior Art Editor Stefan Podhorodecki
Category Publisher Linda Martin
Managing Art Editor Jane Thomas
Picture Researcher Sarah Pownall
DK Picture Library Romaine Werblow
Production Jenny Jacoby
DTP Designer Siu Yin Ho

First published in Great Britain in 2003 by
Dorling Kindersley Limited
80 Strand, London WC2R ORL
A Penguin Company

2 4 6 8 10 9 7 5 3 1

The CIP Catalogue record for this book is available
from the British Library

ISBN 0-7513-3757-9

Reproduced by Colourscan, Singapore
Printed and bound by L.E.G.O., Italy

See our complete
catalogue at
www.dk.com

CONTENTS

INTRODUCTION

Imagine you're running a faint torch beam across the shadowy corner of a dusty attic, or you hear a weird shuffling noise as you tiptoe downstairs at night for a glass of water. Your mind races to one terrifying conclusion – something is waiting for you. And that "something" could be a monster.

Maybe you've never met a monster, or found proof that they exist, but you might be looking in the wrong places. Forget the usual hangouts – graveyards, cellars, lonely roads late at night – and let your imagination run riot. That's exactly where these beasts are lurking.

There's no escape from monsters – not a comforting thought, but true. Monsters live in our imaginations and have been a part of our world for generations. Every culture has created its own monsters, bringing all kinds of bizarre beasts to life in the most fantastic myths and legends.

If you're brave enough to carry on reading this book, you'll find a crazy cross-section of the things that go bump, snarl, and grunt in the night. There are flame-throwing dragons, shape-shifting wizards, and three-headed hounds galore. Enormous giants

tower over tiny elves, crafty
creatures weave a web of trickery, sea
monsters show their terrifying teeth, and
the dead rise from the grave. These tales
aren't just cool, they're positively chilling –
and there's plenty more where they came from.

After mixing with the monsters on these pages,
you may want to pick up a mythology book and read
about the gods, heroes, and other brave men and
women who battled these beasts. Legendary tales
have kept people entertained since practically the
beginning of time, so you know they must be good.

There isn't enough space in this book for all the
monstrosities in mythology. So, if you
want to explore the subject in
more detail, look for the black
Log On "bites" in each chapter.
These will direct you to some
fascinating websites, where
you'll find more on monsters
and their place in the
mythological world.

But first, curl up your toes, chill
your spine, and read on.

MEET THE MONSTERS

People have believed in monsters since (bed)time began. Many old tales feature horrible humans and brutal beasts, who roam through our nightmares and sometimes sneak into our daytime thoughts. These stories are common in every culture and have been used over the years to explain catastrophic events or to demonstrate the power of good over evil.

Prepare to be scared

If you peer into a dark attic or a murky cave it's not hard to imagine something sinister lurking there. But traditional stories (and films) allow you to meet these scary figures from the safety and comfort of your own chair. Whether good or evil, scaly or slimy, tiny or huge, these are the creatures whose strange appearance and powers puts them outside most people's idea of what's real and into the realm of monsters.

NO ONE WANTS TO COME FACE TO FACE WITH A SCALY GREMLIN (A MISCHIEVOUS SPRITE). THIS MALEVOLENT BIG-EARED BEAST IS FROM THE FILM *GREMLINS* (1984).

LOG ON...
www.pantheon.
org/mythica.html

LEGENDS TELL US THAT IN ABOUT 325 BC, ALEXANDER THE GREAT (KING OF MACEDONIA) SAW SEA MONSTERS WHILE EXPLORING THE OCEAN'S DEPTHS IN A GLASS DIVING BELL.

People need monsters

Maybe you don't believe in monsters anymore. You no longer need to check under the bed or at the back of the cupboard to see what might be hiding there. Your own science lessons have probably taught you that there is usually an explanation for everything that happens in nature, and monsters are not part of the equation. So why do so many monster tales exist, in one form or another, in almost every country on earth?

THUNDERBOLTS HAVE BEEN USED AS WEAPONS BY MANY GODS

WEIRD WORLD
THE EARLIEST KNOWN BESTIARY – A COLLECTION OF STORIES ABOUT MONSTERS AND FANTASTIC ANIMALS IN MYTHOLOGY – WAS WRITTEN MORE THAN A THOUSAND YEARS AGO.

To understand why people invented monsters, you need to think back to a time long before you knew it all – before websites, television, and films, books, and school – even before your parents or grandparents were born. Yes, we're talking ancient history.

9

Explaining nature

People who lived long ago didn't have all the answers, but they certainly had questions about their world. For example, people looked at stormy skies and no doubt wanted to know what caused lightning and thunder. Some bright spark, somewhere in the pre-scientific past, came up with an answer that made sense at the time – each zigzag of lightning was a blast of

fire spewed from a dragon's mouth, while a thunderclap was the fierce flapping of its huge wings. The shake of an earthquake had to be the result

THE WEARER OF A FRIGHT MASK IN IROQUOIS HEALING CEREMONIES TOOK ON THE CHARACTER OF A SPIRIT FROM IROQUOI MYTHOLOGY.

of some enormous creature stomping by. A huge tidal wave crashing onto a rocky shore was undoubtedly created by the furious lashing of a sea serpent's tail.

Dark fears

Monsters also came in handy so that people could understand the idea of death. In fact, the leading cause of death in ancient times seemed to be attacks by monsters and other strange mythical beings – at least, that's what plenty of people chose to believe. Blaming a monster for a sudden illness or an unexplained death helped people face their darkest fears about what would happen when their lives came to an end.

Monsters and myths

The tales people once shared about strange creatures were part of a collection of amazing stories called myths (from the Greek word *mythos*, which means "story" or "legend"). Everybody loves a good story, and myths were shared and treasured, passed down through generations of storytellers, and celebrated in art, dance, special ceremonies, poetry, and song.

THIS AFRICAN FETISH FIGURE (A STATUE BELIEVED TO HAVE MAGICAL POWERS TO PROTECT PEOPLE FROM EVIL) REPRESENTS A CHARACTER FROM MYTHOLOGY.

Every society developed its own myths – fantastic tales of creation, stories explaining life and death, legends of divine gods and goddesses, brave and daring heroes, wily tricksters, and many-headed monsters. Today, we still love a good monster story or a fairy tale.

Incredibly, although there was little communication between societies in times gone by (air travel was strictly for the birds), some myths from different cultures were strikingly similar. They had common plots and themes, even the same characters, but with different names. The ancient Egyptians as well as early people in West Africa had myths about a creator shaping

THE GREEK HERO HERACLES BATTLES THE HYDRA, A MULTI-HEADED MONSTER FROM MYTHOLOGY. HERACLES USED THE HYDRA'S BLOOD TO POISON HIS ARROWS.

KILLING THE HYDRA WAS ONE OF THE 12 LABOURS OF HERACLES

humans from clay. Both Japanese and Hindu myths tell how stirring up the seas led to the Earth's creation, and the myths of many cultures feature serpents, giants, or dragons.

The power of myths
Myths were closely connected to a society's religious beliefs, and this made them more

WEIRD WORLD
CHARACTERS FROM MYTHOLOGY LIVED BEYOND THE REACH OF MORTALS – ON TOP OF IMAGINARY MOUNTAINS, INSIDE VOLCANOES, IN VAST UNDERSEA WORLDS, MAZE-LIKE UNDERGROUND CHAMBERS, OR GREAT HALLS IN THE SKY.

important than other stories. While they might have dismissed a folk tale as impossible or silly, people usually considered myths to be true. It was this shared belief that gave myths their power.

In words, pictures, and art
Over the centuries, people found ways to keep myths alive by writing them down, and this is how we found out about them. Myths were collected in different ways. Native Americans recorded theirs on animal skins, Egyptians drew picture writing (hieroglyphs) on tomb walls, Greeks and Romans scratched information into clay tablets, Africans carved mythical figures, and South Americans wove mythical characters into textiles. In the Middle Ages, the people of the British Isles

THIS STATUE TELLS THE ANCIENT STORY OF LAÖCOON AND HIS SONS, WHO SO ANGERED THE GODS THAT THEY SENT TWO SEA SERPENTS TO KILL THEM.

and the Teutonic people of Scandinavia and Germany began writing their myths down in books. Today, people who study mythology can access records from history – and meet more monsters than you might imagine.

New monsters for old

In the last few hundreds of years, scientists have discovered what causes thunder and lightning, hurricanes and tidal waves. But even more monster tales have emerged – stories of blood-sucking vampires, creatures from the murky depths, hairy

THE STAR OF *THE CREATURE FROM THE BLACK LAGOON* – A TYPICAL 1950S LATE-NIGHT HORROR FILM – WAS HALF MAN, HALF FISH.

IN A FUN TWIST ON EARLIER MONSTER FILMS, THE CREATURES IN *MONSTERS INC* ARE TERRIFIED OF CHILDREN.

half-human beasts, mixed-up animals, and scary fairies. Monsters are everywhere, from movies and video games to trading cards and cereal packets. It seems people still need monsters, for some of the same old reasons – to deal with the unknown. And sometimes – let's face it – we like to be scared. As anyone who's a late-night horror-film fan knows, monsters can also be a scream.

DRAGON TALES

D ragons are usually described as fire-breathing, winged monsters, covered in scaly armour from horrible head to stinger-tipped tail. In fact, these creatures get their name from the Greek word, drakon, which means "enormous serpent". In mythology dragons are often forces of evil. They serve a useful purpose by making the mere men who slay them into heroes.

A dragon's lair

Dragons have taken many different forms over time – with or without bat-like wings, with powerful legs or no legs at all, with breath hot as fire or cold as ice. Scarily, dragons have even been described as having more than one red-eyed head. Dragon homes were just as varied. Some lived in caves and mountains, while others made themselves comfortable in swamps and other watery places. Although dragons are often associated with evil, in many cultures they are considered to be friendly.

IN CHINESE MYTHOLOGY A DRAGON REPRESENTS GOOD LUCK

WEIRD WORLD

ACCORDING TO GREEK MYTHOLOGY, THE DRAGON-SHAPED CONSTELLATION, DRACO, WAS FORMED WHEN A GODDESS TOSSED A DRAGON INTO THE SKY, WHERE IT BECAME TRAPPED IN THE STARS.

Dragons' debut

Dragons probably made their first appearance in mythology in the creation stories of

A DRAGON COULD BREATHE OUT FIRE WITH AS MUCH FORCE AS A FLAME THROWER.

ancient Mesopotamia. One 4,000-year-old tale tells that at the beginning of time, Apsu, the god of fresh water, mated with a terrible she-dragon

THE ANCIENT MESOPOTAMIAN DRAGON-SLAYER, MARDUK, KILLED THE DRAGON TIAMAT

named Tiamat. She gave birth to an assortment of horrid monsters that terrorized their father and the other gods. When they'd had enough, the gods persuaded Marduk, the only good kid in the bunch, to challenge his mother and her monstrous offspring to a battle. When he ripped her in two, one half became heaven, the other was Earth, and the blood of his slain siblings became the human race.

In many early cultures, dragons had generally good reputations, and were seen as symbols of power and protective strength. Ancient Egyptians painted dragon images on pyramids and palaces to protect them, in the same way that people might hang up a "beware of dog" sign today.

The emperor's emblem

Dragons were definitely top dogs in ancient China, loved and revered by the people as well as their rulers, who chose dragons as symbols of the imperial throne. In fact, if you wanted to compliment an emperor in ancient China, you'd call him "dragon face". Chinese myths tell of serpent-like, wingless dragons, friendly

THE DRAGON OF NORSE MYTHOLOGY, REPRESENTED HERE BY A VIKING ARTEFACT, WAS A SYMBOL OF EVIL. IT ATE CORPSES AND GNAWED AT THE TREE OF LIFE.

and wise, who controlled the rain, rivers, lakes, and seas – especially important during the crop-growing season. Dragons are still considered lucky in China. This is why every Lunar New Year's parade features a team of dragon dancers weaving their way through the streets in a dragon costume, to keep evil away for another year.

When good dragons go bad

In the mythology of many other cultures, dragons didn't exactly keep evil away – they couldn't, because they were incredibly evil themselves. What happened? People wanted heroes, and heroes had

THE HIGHLIGHT OF A CHINESE NEW YEAR PARADE IS THE DRAGON DANCE. SOME OF THE SILK, BAMBOO, AND PAPER CREATIONS STRETCH AS FAR AS 30 M (100 FT).

19

THE DRAGON, WITH ITS FIERY BREATH, RED-RIMMED EYES, AND MOUTHFUL OF HIDEOUS TEETH, IS ONE OF THE BEST-KNOWN CREATURES IN MONSTER WORLD.

to do heroic things — such as single-handedly slaying a hideous dragon. And what if that dragon was guarding an enormous hoard of treasure? Bonus hero points would definitely be awarded.

These sorts of dragon tales cropped up everywhere. In Norse (Scandinavian) myth, a hero named Sigurd slaughtered a fire-breathing dragon named Fafnir, who just happened to be coiled up on a pile of treasure. Sigurd took a bath in the dead dragon's blood, which made him unconquerable (and also in dire need of another bath).

Apollo was a superhero of

THIS DRAGON-SLAYER'S HELMET WAS RECOVERED FROM A 7TH-CENTURY SHIP BURIAL AT SUTTON HOO IN SUFFOLK.

Greek mythology, who used a bow and arrow to kill a terrible dragon named Python. This snake-like creature had caused havoc throughout the land.

B eowulf the bold

One of the most exciting dragon tales is the 8th-century epic poem, named after its hero, Beowulf.

A noble warrior of Northern Europe, Beowulf had slain three fearsome monsters in his youth. As an old man he was challenged once more by a horrid fire-breathing dragon, which was hoarding a fantastic treasure trove. This same dragon was also burning down the surrounding farms and villages, one big, bad breath at a time.

After a mighty battle, Beowulf managed to thrust his sword into the dragon's jaw, causing a fatal wound. Yet, as he struggled to pull out the weapon, poisonous goo dripped down from the dragon's mouth, killing the brave old king.

G ood knights

Tales of dragon slaying were especially popular in the Middle Ages (the period between AD 500 and 1500). In those days, treasure wasn't the only thing at stake – a knight often battled a terrifying dragon to win the heart of a fair maiden. One of the most famous stories is the English legend of St George and the dragon. George was a Roman soldier who had converted to

THE BIG BAD MONSTER GETS A LANCE RIGHT IN THE EYE IN THIS PAINTING BY PAOLO UCCELLO (1397–1475), DEPICTING BRAVE ST GEORGE SLAYING THE DRAGON.

deed that made him the patron saint of England.

Dragons on the rooftops

In medieval France, people told tales of the gargouille ("gargler"), a dragon that spat out huge torrents of water instead of fire. A bishop took away the dragon's powers with the sign of the cross, and from then on, gargoyles (sculptures in the form of monsters) were put on cathedrals and other buildings as symbols of protection. They were usually used as spouts on the roof gutters, so that excess rain would gush out through their open mouths.

A GROTESQUE GARGOYLE USUALLY SITS ON ITS HAUNCHES, PEERING DOWN FROM A BUILDING.

A GARGOYLE IS USUALLY A GROTESQUE BIRD OR BEAST

the Christian faith. Like a medieval exterminator, he came to the aid of a town that had a real dragon problem. This neighbourhood bully was wrecking homes and farms (after eating up all the animals). The king decided to sacrifice his own daughter to try to stop the rampaging dragon. George rode in on a white horse, killed the dragon, and rescued the damsel in distress – a noble

Modern dragons

The brave knights obviously didn't vanquish all the dragons, because they are now more popular than ever. Japanese horror movies and graphic novels are chock-a-block with dragons. The granddaddy of them all is Godzilla, the vast and nearly invincible dragon-like monster who regularly drops by Japan to stomp, crush, and destroy everything in sight.

Fans of the Harry Potter books are familiar with the dragon hatching – and smuggling – that Harry and his mates get up to, while the fantasy game Dungeons and Dragons claims to be the world's most popular role-playing game.

A live and kicking

Scientists have even found a real dragon – well, almost. In 1912, a pilot returning from a trip to Komodo (a volcanic island in Indonesia) swore he had found dragons on the island. He claimed that they devoured goats and pigs and even attacked larger animals such as horses. Many people suspected the pilot had been in the sun for too long, but the hunt to capture a real dragon was on. In 1926, two live komodo dragons were brought to a zoo in New York City, where they caused a sensation. Today, you can take a look at these vulnerable dragons in zoos around the world.

THE WORLD'S LARGEST LIZARD, THE KOMODO DRAGON IS A FEARSOME PREDATOR, CAPABLE OF EATING A HUMAN.

LOG ON...
Here be dragons
www.draconia.com

SERPENTS AND SEA MONSTERS

S limy, scaly, or slithery, aquatic monsters have wriggled their way into the mythology of almost every culture. If you dive into their watery world, you'll discover the difference between serpent and saurian, and meet some of the top lake, river, and sea monsters.

Wet and wild

Most mythological water monsters fall into one of two categories – serpent or saurian. Serpents are generally depicted as marine (sea) creatures, with long, slinky bodies that could easily stretch to a boat length or two. Although they make their homes at sea, a trip to the beach – beyond – is within their reach. Most sea serpents are covered in scaly, dark-co   skin that provides camouflage in the rolling waves. Their snake-like heads are flat and blunt (the perfect shape for tipping over a boatload of

AN OLD ENGRAVING SHOWS A SAILING SHIP IN THE SLIMY CLUTCHES OF A LARGER-THAN-LIFE GIANT SQUID.

sailors at
lunchtime).
They are
sometimes adorned
with pointy horns, dangling
whiskers, giant nostrils,
forked tongues, or a jawful
of scary fangs. In short, they
have faces only mother sea
monsters could love.

Fins, flippers, and feet
help most seaworthy
serpents stay in the swim.
But some creatures have
none, relying instead on the
swish of a tail or a thrashing
tentacle to move about. What
most distinguishes sea serpents
is their swimming style. These
creatures use an up-and-down
motion to slide through the
sea. Sometimes, bits of their

EVEN TODAY, DIVERS CAN
FIND THEMSELVES FACE
TO FACE WITH A GIANT
OCTOPUS 5 M (16 FT) LONG.

A SAILOR'S WORST FEAR WAS TO BE GOBBLED UP BY A SEA SERPENT AFTER A SHIPWRECK, AS SHOWN IN THIS PAINTING.

bodies break the surface as they swim, giving the impression that they have humped backs.

Dinosaur cousins

Saurian water monsters are related to their extinct reptile cousins – dinosaurs named plesiosaurs. Both names come from a Greek word meaning "lizard". A typical saurian in mythology looks a bit like an overgrown seahorse. Its barrel-shaped body has a tapering tail at one end, and a long, curving neck topped with a small "horsey" head at the other. Almost all saurians have flippers, and many are shown with stubby, snail-like horns sticking out from their monstrous foreheads.

Most saurian monsters in mythology live in large, deep lakes, surfacing now and again to take a breath. You might smell a saurian before you see it, because pond scum and bits of rotting plant and animal matter are often attached to the beast's slippery hide, giving off a horribly obnoxious odour.

WEIRD WORLD
THE LEGEND OF AMERICA'S ALKALI LAKE MONSTER SAYS ITS STENCH IS ENOUGH TO KILL YOU. IF THAT DOESN'T WORK, TAKING IN THE MONSTER'S AWFUL APPEARANCE WILL DO THE TRICK, BLEACHING YOUR HAIR AND CRACKING YOUR BRAIN.

Terror in the sea

A closer look at some legendary sea serpents will show you that these snakes weren't very likeable. Ancient Hebrew legends tell of a terrible serpent called Leviathan, able to unleash incredible evil and chaos. The monster was said to be so immense that the sea boiled whenever it surfaced. Even the sharpest spears and harpoons failed to pierce its incredibly tough hide, bouncing off pathetically into the sea. To make matters worse smoke billowed out from the creature's nostrils, and flames shot out of its mouth.

Beastly beasts

You'd really need to get your head together to battle the Hydra. This serpent from Greek mythology was notorious not only for its putrid breath, which tainted the waters around it, but also for its many heads. The Hydra had at least seven heads. If one was lopped off, two more would grow in its place. The legendary Greek hero Heracles bravely disposed of the beast by slashing off each of its heads and setting fire to the stump before new ones could sprout. A daring hero might think he stood a better chance against the Norse serpent, Nidhogg – that is, until he found out that its name translates to "tearer of corpses." Not only did it gnaw at the tree of life itself, but it fed on corpses in Niflheim, the realm of the dead.

Lambton worm

Legend holds that a vile black worm, or serpent, terrorized the people of a small village. This was England's famous Lambton

LOG ON...
Check out the monster
www.lochness.co.uk

THIS BRONZE STATUE BY GIAMBOLOGNA (1529–1608) SHOWS HERACLES IN THE FINAL STAGES OF SLASHING OFF THE HEADS OF THE MONSTROUS HYDRA.

IN THIS ENGRAVING, THE NORSE GOD THOR ATTEMPTS TO KILL A SEA SERPENT (SO HUGE IT ENCIRCLES THE GLOBE) WITH HIS MAGIC HAMMER.

Worm, which was accidentally fished from the River Wear by an unfortunate fisherman. The Worm was a curious-looking, completely black serpent that oozed sticky slime from its pores. The horrified fisherman tossed the creature into a well on his way back home. In no time, odd smells began drifting from the well, and villagers were appalled to see the monster's slimy tracks leading back to the river.

Before long the worm turned, eating whole sheep in one gulp, ripping open cows' udders with razor-sharp teeth to get to the milk, and dismembering anyone who came too close. Not surprisingly, the villagers learned to leave the worm alone, but something had to be done. The fisherman, now a knight, decided to do the right thing, and devised a suit of armour coated with lethal double-edged spikes. When the worm lunged at him, the spikes tore its flesh off a chunk at a time. The monster became so weak that it was easily finished off with a bop on the head.

Slithering saurians

Mythological monsters obviously like to be beside the seaside, but deep, seemingly bottomless lakes are also excellent haunts, especially for saurians. Ever since Native Americans lived on the shores of Lake Champlain (on the border of New England and Canada), there have been tales – and repeated sightings – of a monster nicknamed Champ. This saurian is said to be huge, with water-slick grey skin, a humped back, and glowing green eyes. In Champ's "youth", in the 1800s, local farmers blamed the monster for incidents of missing livestock, but it is now considered to be harmless.

Nessie

Of course, the world's most famous watery wonder is the Loch Ness Monster.

Tucked into the highlands of Scotland, Loch Ness is pretty remarkable in itself. At 32 km (20 miles) long and up to 2.4 km (1.5 miles) wide, it is Britain's largest freshwater lake. The waters are cold and very murky, crisscrossed with dangerous currents – in fact, it is a perfect place for a monster to hide. As early as the 6th century, someone wrote a story about rescuing an unfortunate person from the jaws of a monster in the loch. From time to time rumours of something hungry lurking in the lake reappeared. After a road was constructed around the loch in the 1930s, monster sightings increased dramatically.

The Loch Ness Monster, or Nessie, is described as about 9.1 m (30 ft) in length, with a long, tapering neck and a large hump in its back. Before long, the first fuzzy "photographs" of

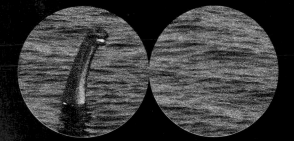

IN THE MURKY DEPTHS OF LOCH NESS, WHICH IS 183 M (600 FT)) DEEP, DIVERS USE AN UNDERWATER CAMERA TO SEARCH FOR NESSIE. THE PHOTO (RIGHT) IS THOUGHT TO BE FAKE.

Nessie were revealed. Although these were later found to be fakes, something about this creature captured the public's imagination, and the quest was on. Over the years, scientists have prodded the depths of the loch with sonar equipment, underwater cameras – even a small submarine – but Nessie remains camera-shy.

29

FLYING MONSTERS

From enormous eagles to oversized owls, and huge bats to supernatural bees, an amazing array of airborne creatures soars through the skies, winging their way into myth and legend. Some foretell bad news or act as deadly messengers for the gods, while others represent the awesome power of nature. Whatever their role, these winged weirdos are probably popular in mythology because the power of flight seems so magical to those of us who are stuck firmly on the ground.

Flesh-eating bird

Strange stories of giant birds are found throughout world mythology. Arabian legends tell of the monstrous bird as a sign that something nasty was about to happen. If you saw this bird fly overhead, you knew that a terrible battle or a bad harvest was on the way.

IN MYTHOLOGY, THE FEATHERS OF SOME BIRDS SPELL BAD LUCK

called Roc, who had a taste for elephants, which it clutched in its sharp talons and carried back to its nest. For pudding, Roc was fond of nibbling dead human flesh from the battlefields. Not surprisingly, Roc was regarded

THE NATIVE AMERICANS MADE WOODEN CARVINGS OF THEIR FLYING TERROR, THE THUNDERBIRD.

of its massive wings as it flew through the skies was said to bring a shattering thunderclap and gale-force winds. The monster could make lightning simply by blinking its eyes. The Thunderbird was usually portrayed as a human-gobbling nightmare, but in other stories, the creature was kind and helpful. In one tale, the Thunderbird saved the lives of a starving tribe by picking up a whale in its claws and dropping it off for the people to feast on.

Tribes in the American southwest were terrified of Big Owl, a gigantic beast with white feathers, glowing eyes, and a taste for tribespeople. Big Owl ruled the night skies, its snowy form outlined against the full

THE LEGENDARY BIRD OF PREY ROC DIGS ITS TERRIBLE TALONS INTO AN ELEPHANT'S FLESH AND CARRIES IT OFF.

Thunderbird and Big Owl

Native American tribes of the Pacific Northwest and the Great Lakes told stories about the Thunderbird, a huge creature with feathers as long as canoe paddles and talons the size of a human arm. Each flap

WEIRD WORLD
ACCORDING TO ARABIC TRADITION, THE GREAT BIRD ROC NEVER LANDS ON EARTH, BUT ONLY ON THE MOUNTAIN QAF, WHICH LIES AT THE CENTRE OF THE WORLD.

THE MONSTROUS BIG OWL
HUNTS ITS PREY BY
THE LIGHT OF A
FULL MOON.

Moon for one horrifying instant before it snatched up its prey on a one-way trip to its mountaintop home.

Fine-feathered friends

Not all birds in mythology are terrors. The Firebird is a star of Russian folklore, its feathers shining like silver and gold and its eyes sparkling like crystals. The Firebird's glow was said to be as bright as a thousand lights. Its diet of golden apples gave it miraculous powers too. When a Firebird sang, the sick were healed, and the blind could see. As an added touch of glamour, pearls dropped from its beak with each note.

Chinese mythology tells of a fabulous bird called Feng Huang, which had a pheasant's head and peacock's tail. Its

to place an offering of an egg on the altar of the Sun god.

Other winged things

Mythical birds shared their airspace with a host of other flying creatures, such as bats, bees, moths, and dragonflies. Throughout Western mythology, bats are often linked with death. In China, however, bats are symbols of good fortune and happiness, perhaps because the word for bat, "fu," sounds like the word for good luck. Their bad reputation no doubt comes from the fact that bats are creatures of the night.

Some stories probably don't help the bat's image either. Australian Aboriginal peoples

tail feathers were said to contain the multi-coloured lights of paradise, while its five-note call rang out in sweet and perfect harmony. The Chinese musical scale is said to be based on the melodic call of the Feng Huang.

One of the most magical birds in mythology is the Phoenix, from both ancient Greek and Egyptian tales. Only one Phoenix could exist at any given time. It spent its days near a well, where its morning song was so beautiful it stopped the passing Sun god's chariot in its tracks. At night, it fed upon the light of the stars. When the creature believed its death was near, it built itself a nest of frankincense (scented tree resin) and aromatic twigs, and burst into flames. The Phoenix was then reborn from the ashes, rising up to the city of the Sun

THE MYTHICAL BIRD PHOENIX, SOMETIMES KNOWN AS THE FIREBIRD, PREPARES TO SET ITSELF ALIGHT IN A NEST OF FIRE.

WEIRD WORLD
THE POMO TRIBE OF CALIFORNIA
BELIEVED THAT BATS CHEWED UP
VOLCANIC ROCK AND SPAT OUT
PERFECT ARROWHEADS TO
TOP THEIR SPEARS.

IN MYTH AND
LEGEND, HANGING
AROUND WITH A BAT
COULD BE SEEN AS AN
OMEN OF DEATH.

Magical bug
The beautiful dragonfly has special meaning for many cultures, sometimes mixing good and bad qualities. For example, in China it's a sign of

believe that the first inhabitants of the land, a man and a woman, were warned by a higher being to keep away from a huge bat perched in front of a cave. Over time, the woman became desperate to find out what the bat was hiding in the cave. When she approached, the bat flew from its perch, releasing death into the world. From that day onwards, death was inevitable for humans.

LOG ON...
www.dur.ac.uk/Grey
College/art/dyson/mythology.htm

IN GREEK LEGENDS, A SWARM OF CLOSELY GUARDED SACRED BEES MADE SPECIAL HONEY TO NOURISH THE GODS.

until they are calmed down by a holy man – the ancient version of pest control.

B uzzy tales

Bees also feature in mythology. In stories from ancient Greece, it was their job to collect nectar – the drink of the gods, which rained down from the heavens each morning as dew. But the buzz on these creatures wasn't all good. The Egyptian Sun god, Ra, was said to weep tears of bees. In European mythology, bees were seen as messengers to the gods, sent to break the bad news that a human had died. Distrust of these winged stingers was such that a swarm of bees landing on a dead tree was thought to signify death and disaster.

summer, but also of weakness. Dragonflies hold a special place in Native American mythology. The Zuni people believe that these creatures have magical powers. In the mythology of the Navajo, dragonflies are regarded as harmful,

A FIERCE HUNTER OF WATER INSECTS AND BABY FISH, THE DRAGONFLY COMBINES BEAUTY WITH THE KILLER INSTINCT,

BEES PUT THE STING IN MANY ANCIENT TALES.

35

TRICKSTER TALES

Monsters aren't always violent – many of the creatures in myth and legend enjoy a little mischief as well. These cunning characters are known as tricksters, because they like to play tricks. Sometimes depicted as animals, with special skills or supernatural powers, tricksters can also take on human forms. Many of them exist to have fun, but some use a talent for twisting the truth to cause chaos in the world.

Animal antics

Various types of animals make an appearance in trickster myths, from creepy crawlies to cunning hares. The Ashanti people of West Africa spin wild tales of a spider trickster named Anansi. He could easily outwit other animals, people, and even the gods. According to legend, Anansi's special job during the creation of the world was delivering wishes and prayers from the Ashanti people to their supreme god, Nyame. The sly spider worked wonders. When the people moaned about working all day long, he persuaded Nyame to create

THE TENGU ARE TRICKSTERS FROM JAPAN – PART BIRD, PART MAN

nights, as a time of rest. A grumble about general weather conditions led to the invention of the Sun to heat the day, the Moon to light up the night – and the wind and rain to provide variety. But Anansi had a crafty streak, and although he had brought good things to so many, there was something he definitely wanted for himself – Nyame's box of sacred (holy) stories.

convinced the snake that it was longer than he was. As the python slithered up alongside the tree, Anansi tied the trunk and the snake together with some vines. Next, he caught the leopard in a deep pit covered with leaves and

THE SPIDER ANANSI WATCHES PATIENTLY AS THE HORNETS BUZZ THEIR WAY INTO THE GOURD THAT HE HAS SET UP TO TRICK THEM.

Spider stories

Nyame put the eight-legged trickster to the test by offering to release the stories if Anansi could complete a nearly impossible task – to capture a giant python, a leopard with teeth like spears, an angry hive of hornets, and a mysterious fairy. First, Anansi took a tree trunk to the python's lair, and

branches – an old trick, but a good one. Then Anansi hollowed out a gourd and filled it with water. He approached the hornets and tipped the water over himself so that they thought it was raining. They buzzed into the gourd for shelter – just as Anansi banged down the lid. Finally, he trapped the fairy by making a doll from sticky tar. As soon as she gave her new friend a hug, she was stuck fast. Nyame was

37

THIS AFRICAN MASK WAS WORN TO IMPERSONATE HARE, OR BRER RABBIT, WHO IS SEEN CLIMBING UP THE SIDE OF IT.

impressed, so that he handed the sacred box of tales to Anansi. These spider stories have now become an essential part of African mythology.

Hare or Brer Rabbit

Other African trickster myths feature the adventures of Hare. This animal was no dumb bunny, but he was a bit lazy, using his active mind to make up for a less-than-active body. For example, when it was crop-planting season, Hare challenged an elephant and a hippopotamus to a game of tug of war. As the big beasts slid back and forth across the earth, they cleared the field for planting, while Hare put his big

feet up. When African slaves were taken to America, they took with them the stories of Hare and other animals, making them part of African-American folklore. In America, Hare was known as Brer Rabbit.

Coyote

In many legends of the Native American people, especially the tribes of the Southwest and the Great Plains, the ultimate trickster is Coyote. Like other mischief makers, his tricks can be funny or tragic. He is sometimes described as the creator of humans, but in other tales, the only thing he creates is chaos.

Coyote appears in many forms – as a man, an animal, or an invisible power able to change the direction of rivers and move mountains. Whatever form he takes, Coyote has enough curiosity to get him into big trouble – but enough cunning to get him out again. In one story, Coyote disturbed the creator, who was baking clay into the first people. As the creator shooed Coyote away, he forgot what was cooking in his oven. Some people turn out medium rare,

WEIRD WORLD

THE NATIVE AMERICAN TRICKSTER TAQWUS GAVE OFF A SHOWER OF BIZARRE BLUE SPARKS AS HE CARRIED OUT HIS DAILY MORNING TASK – STEALING PEOPLE'S SOULS.

while others were well done. So, thanks to Coyote, people come in many different colours.

One of Coyote's arch enemies was another Native American trickster, Raven. After one of his pranks misfired, this bird was booted out of heaven, and the frantic flapping of its wings caused land to rise from the oceans, creating our world. When he wasn't being hounded by Coyote, Raven was stealing the Sun and the Moon and hanging them in the sky.

B ad dogs and ponies

Some legendary animals are bad all the way through. One example is Barghest, a

monster dog from Yorkshire who moved silently through the night and could appear and disappear at will. The only clue to its presence was the clicking of its terrible claws, and the gnashing of its huge teeth. If you were unlucky enough to see the dog clearly, you might as well proceed directly to the graveyard, as your death would be inevitable.

It would be slightly safer to encounter the shaggy, harmless-looking pony from

COYOTE'S CUNNING IS CELEBRATED IN THE BEADWORK MOTIF OF THIS NATIVE AMERICAN SHIELD.

As he grew to an enormous size – with strength to match – he broke through one set of chains after another. The gods asked the magical dwarves to make a special chain that could not be broken. And so they made one, from six invisible things – a cat's footsteps, fish breath, the roots of a mountain, bird spittle, the sinews of a bear, and a woman's beard. Amazingly, the ribbon-thin chain worked, and Fenrir was tied to a rock for ever more.

Irish legend, called Phooka. Yet if you climbed on for a ride, this beast would unleash its full fury, charging to hell and back through thorn bushes and muddy marshes before tossing you into the deepest ditch.

Wicked wolf

One of the most beastly baddies in all mythology is Fenrir, the giant wolf of Norse legend. Although he was no trouble as a little wolf, the gods heard a prophecy that a wolf would be responsible for the destruction of the world. So, they decided to chain up Fenrir and keep a close eye on him.

Maui-of-a-thousand-tricks

Not all of these cunning characters are animals. The trickster hero, Maui, lived in Polynesia, the triangular area that includes Hawaii, Easter Island, and New Zealand. Maui wasn't content to accept things as they were. When his mother complained that she couldn't fit enough hours into the day, he caught the Sun as it sped by, in a noose made from his sister's hair. Then he beat up the Sun

LOG ON…
pjmichaels/glorantha/foolsparadise.htm
members.aol.com/

with his grandmother's magic jawbone until it promised to slow its journey across the sky, making daytime last a little bit longer.

Maui was also an incredible fisherman. In one story, his brothers refused to share their bait with him on a fishing trip, so Maui used his blood to reel in his biggest catch – the North Island of New Zealand. The native people of New Zealand, the Maori, call the North Island Te Ika a Maui (the fish of Maui).

B lack and white

Another trickster from West African mythology, Eshu appeared as a human in several different sizes. His wisdom and grasp of languages made him a natural go-between for the gods and their people. Yet Eshu also loved to confuse people, sometimes driving them to the point of madness. In one tale, the tricky character wore a hat that was black on one side and

THIS MAORI CARVING SHOWS POLYNESIAN TRICKSTER MAUI REELING IN A FISH THAT REPRESENTS NEW ZEALAND.

white on the other. People who saw him argued furiously about the colour of his hat. If only they could have seen both sides of it.

C heeky chap

The Egyptian god Bes caused more laughter than chaos. This little man, with bowed legs and shaggy hair, had a cheeky face and love of music. He stuck out his tongue in the face of danger, and banged together the tools in his tiny hands to ward off evil. Statues of Bes stood in every ancient Egyptian home.

IN THIS AFRICAN STATUE OF ESHU, HE HOLDS A TINY STATUE OF HIMSELF OVER ONE SHOULDER.

MONSTER MIX

Mythology is full of tales about the marriages of different creatures, which resulted in a wild mix of monsters, both male and female. There are strange mergers between humans and animals, as well as crazy beasts made from different animal features. Other monsters have something extra – more heads, arms, or legs for instance. Most are mad, bad, and extremely dangerous.

Three-headed horror

In Greek mythology, the entrance to Hades, the realm of the dead, was guarded by a demonic dog named Cerberus. This three-headed horror was happy to let souls of the dead enter Hades, but none was allowed to come out. However, a few people did manage to sneak by the barking beast. The hero Orpheus put the dog to sleep with a little lyre music, then made his escape. In Roman legends the Trojan prince Aeneas got on the creature's good side with a honey-flavoured dog biscuit.

Half bull, half man
Another Greek monster was the Minotaur, who had the head and tail of a bull and the body of a man. The story began when Minos sought to become ruler of the island of Crete. He asked the gods to send him a special bull, which he would then sacrifice to show his devotion. When he saw the magnificent beast, Minos wanted it for himself, so he swapped one of his own herd

THE DEMON DOG CERBERUS BARES ITS TERRIFYING TEETH. ITS SERPENT'S TAIL HISSES AT ANYONE OR ANYTHING THAT TRIES TO APPROACH.

for the sacrifice. The gods guessed Minos' sneaky trick, and decided to punish him by making his wife fall madly in love with the bull. She built a wooden cow suit, climbed in, and a few months later the Minotaur was born.

Being bull-headed, the Minotaur spread terror and a trail of destruction across Crete. Minos asked the architect Daedalus to create a labyrinth, a maze-like prison from which there could be no escape, and the Minotaur was locked inside.

Every year the king tossed a few children into the labyrinth to feed the beast. However, when a hero from Athens named Theseus heard about this dreadful sacrifice, he was determined to slay the creature. With the help of the king's daughter, he made a plan. He took a ball of string into the maze, unrolling it as he went, until he came upon the sleeping beast. Theseus then beat it to death and followed the string path back, out of the labyrinth, to safety.

S trange and scaly
Another common mythological mix was a cross

THE MONSTROUS MINOTAUR
KNEW EVERY TWIST AND TURN
OF THE LABYRINTH.

between a human and a serpent, no doubt due to the snake's long-lived association with evil. One of these creatures, named Typhon, was among the scariest, ugliest monsters of all time (his hideous half-nymph, half-snake wife Echidna takes second place). Even the gods hid when Typhon appeared.

His head crashed into the stars, venom dripped from his awful eyes, and bubbling hot lava poured from his mouth. His lower body was encircled with snakes, and instead of fingertips, he had a hundred hissing serpents. The gods struggled with Typhon for years. Then someone had the clever idea of trapping him under the volcanic Mt Etna in Italy, where he is said to remain to this day, spewing out fire and molten rock.

S nakey sisters

Every day was a bad hair day for the Gorgons, three monsters with snakes instead of hair. (These hair-raising creatures were called Gorgonyou in Russian folk tales.) Some Greek myths say that Medusa, one of the Gorgons, was originally a pretty but vain girl. She made

45

the mistake of boasting that her hair was more beautiful than any goddess' locks, and in an instant her hair became a mass of slithering snakes. Anyone who dared to look at her was instantly turned to stone. The Greek hero Perseus finally managed to lop off her head, by looking at her reflection in a bronze shield as he gave Medusa her last-ever haircut.

THIS SO-CALLED MERMAID SKELETON, CAPTURED BY SAILORS AT SEA, IS IN FACT A SKATE, A TYPE OF FLAT FISH.

L amia

Just as monstrous was Lamia, who had the body of a snake, the head and chest of a woman, and the diet of a vampire. Her treat was to catch young children and drink their blood.

Ancient Greek myths say that Lamia was a princess who fell in love with the already-married top god, Zeus. His jealous wife turned Lamia into a monster and killed her children for revenge. In a horrible twist, she made sure Lamia's eyes couldn't close, so that she was forever sleepless, tormented by images of her children. Zeus later gave Lamia the ability to pluck out her own eyes so that she could escape the full horror of her vision. But her only comfort was to steal other people's children.

F ish people

If you delve deep into mythology, you will haul in a huge catch of half-human sea creatures. A Triton, for example, had a man's head and torso and the tail of a fish. He used magic seahorses and sea monsters like jet skis to zip across the world's oceans, occasionally sounding a blast through his conch-shell to control the ocean waves.

Many sailor's tales tell of an encounter with a mermaid, a fantastic creature with the head and upper body of a beautiful woman and the lower body of a fish. There are mermaid legends all over the globe – in India, these creatures are known as Apsara, and Japanese myths tell of mermaid-like creatures called Ninyo. When mermaids aren't swimming the seas, they are sunning themselves on the rocks, combing their long hair while singing strange songs to lure sailors to the rocky coast.

According to myth, the mermaids took their enchanted prisoners down to the bottom of the sea, where they lived in a fabulous watery kingdom with mermen and merchildren. Because of this story, many sailors saw mermaids as terrible omens of death by drowning.

One of the strangest crosses between sea creature and land lubber is the yara-ma-yha-who, a monster from the aboriginal people of Australia. This creature was a child-sized, bright red man, with a huge head and mouth, and octopus suckers instead of fingertips and toes. The beast used its powerful suckers to hold down human prey as it drank most of their blood.

LOG ON...
www.monstrous.com/galleries.htm

Winged terrors

Many cultures have hatched incredible tales of half-human, half-bird creatures. The Harpies, or robbers, were winged women, equipped with huge, crooked talons, who swooped down from the skies to snatch up a terrified victim. The Harpies then carried their catches to the underworld for a spot of torture, and they were never seen again.

In Hindu mythology, the king of the birds was Garuda, who had a human body with an

THIS OLD ENGRAVING SHOWS A HUNGRY HARPY SINKING HER CROOKED CLAWS INTO HER LATEST UNFORTUNATE VICTIM.

47

eagle's beak and wings. This creature's skin and feathers were a brilliant gold, which shone bright as the Sun. Garuda soared through the skies, ridden by the great god Vishnu, helping to wipe out evil (while occasionally scooping up a snake for dinner in its clawed feet).

Other winged creatures from Greek mythology were Sirens, who had women's heads perched on top of bird bodies. They lived on a rocky island,

often fatal. Some sailors came up with ways to avoid the sirens' calls – drowning them out with loud music, or filling everyone's ears with wax.

R iddles and poison darts

Humans have always been impressed by a lion's incredible strength, and there are stories about lion and human crosses throughout mythology. Among the most famous of these creatures is the Sphinx. In ancient Egypt, this creature

THE SPHINX DEVOURED MEN WHO GOT THE RIDDLE WRONG

where their charming music lured ships ever closer. When the sirens raised their voices in song, no sailor could resist – even though the results were

WITH SUCH A PUZZLING APPEARANCE – A WOMAN'S HEAD ON A LION'S BODY – IT'S NO WONDER A SPHINX LOVED RIDDLES.

appears as a lion with a human head. In statues and wall paintings of the time, it is shown wearing a royal headdress. In Greek mythology, the Sphinx was a winged lion with a woman's head. She sat on a rock at the entrance to the town of Thebes, posing a riddle to all who passed. She asked which creature has one voice, but goes by four legs in the morning, two in the afternoon, and three in the evening? Anyone who couldn't give the answer was eaten.

Finally, the Greek hero Oedipus came up with the answer (it's man, who crawls on all fours as a baby, walks on two legs as an adult, and hobbles with a cane during the twilight of his life) and the enraged lion lady threw herself to her death.

A similar beast, the manticore, is said to roam the forests of Asia, where it is considered one of the deadliest predators ever. This lion has a human face, with three rows of savage teeth. Its tail is tipped with poison darts for zapping prey and causing instant death. Then the creature eats all of its victim, including its clothes, bones, hair, spare change, bus pass, and whatever else it can find.

Beastly lions

There are enough strange mixed-up animals in mythology to populate a small, and extremely odd, zoo. Up in the air, you might spot winged elephants from Hindu mythology or flying bulls and leopards from Babylonian tales. On the ground, you could encounter bulls with scales or giant golden horns, nine-tailed foxes or eight-legged horses, snakes with heads at both ends of their bodies — even a cross between a rooster and a lizard .

The griffin was one such jumbled-up creature, with the head, beak, and wings of an eagle, the body of a lion, and a

HALF BIRD, HALF LION, GRIFFINS ARE THE TRUSTED GUARDIANS OF GOLD AND OTHER VALUABLES IN MYTHOLOGY.

serpent for a tail. But this beast was more than the sum of its parts – it was stronger than 12 eagles, and fiercer than an entire pack of lions. Its origins were in Middle Eastern mythology, but griffin-like creatures were found in legends across the globe. One of their favourite games was swooping down on a horse and rider, and carrying them both off.

The Chimera was another botched-up lion. This fire-breathing monster had the head and front paws of a lion, with the head and neck of a female goat on its back, and a lizard-like rear end with a serpent for a tail. With three mouths to feed, it's not surprising that this creature loved killing and eating people. It was eventually slain by a Greek hero named Bellerophon, who just happened to be riding by on the winged horse Pegasus.

Hybrid horses

Not all cross breeds, or so-called hybrids, in mythology are monsters. Pegasus was a magical horse, with a pair of white feathery wings on his back and a golden bridle around his neck. Born from

SOME MYTHS SAY THE CHIMERA BREATHES FIRE – BUT THEY DON'T SAY FROM WHICH OF ITS THREE HORRIFYING HEADS THE FLAMES SHOOT OUT.

the blood of the decapitated, snake-haired Medusa, this winged wonder was the loyal companion of Bellerophon. After killing the Chimera, Bellerophon was so

PEGASUS FLEW UP TO HEAVEN AND BECAME A GROUP OF STARS

puffed up with pride that he attempted to ride Pegasus all the way to heaven. Pegasus knew this was forbidden, so he tossed his rider into the sky.

Another hybrid horse in mythology is the unicorn, a pure white beast with a single, spiral-shaped horn sticking out of its forehead. In western mythology, the unicorn was seen as wild and untamable. In Asia – where the creature is named kirin – these beasts were shy, gentle, and kind. They

were also said to bring good luck to those who caught sight of them or touched them. A unicorn's horn was believed to have incredible cleansing and healing powers. Just one dip of a horn into a poisoned lake made the water pure again, and a pinch of dust from the horn worked better than any medicine to fight disease. In heraldry, this gentle beast has a twisted horn, a deer's feet, a goat's beard, and a lion's tail – the classic monster mix.

HUGE AND HAIRY

Looking like a crazy cross between human and ape, hairy monsters from Bigfoot to the Yeti are believed to roam the wilds of the world. Every culture seems to claim at least one hairy apeman as its own, and the appearance and behaviour of these legendary creatures is strikingly similar. They are usually spotted in high mountainous areas or in deep swamps, and often leave a tell-tale trail of footprints and a zoo-cage smell.

Hair everywhere

If you comb through mythology books, you'll find that all these creatures, from small to tall, hate haircuts. Many legends describe them as covered in hair, with a few bare patches around the eyes, nose, and ears, as well as the soles of the feet and palms of the hands. Most are dark-haired, but redheads, blondes, and grey- and silver-maned monsters feature as well. Some tales tell of glowing eyes, able to see out of the facial fuzz.

These heavily hairy beasts are found in small, medium, and large sizes, with the biggest ones said to reach an incredible 3.6 m (12 ft) tall, and weighing in at half a tonne. A creature such as this could easily uproot a tree or a telephone pole with a single tug.

BIGFOOT IS A VERY LARGE, HIRSUTE, BIPEDAL HOMINID!

Hairy hominids are often described as loners, content to stomp around remote areas – from mountaintops to swamp bottoms,

THIS CREATURE, BASED ON THE DESCRIPTIONS OF BIGFOOT, WAS THE STAR OF THE MOVIE *BIGFOOT AND THE HENDERSONS*.

occasionally letting out a spine-chilling howl.

Tibetan terror
It's hardly surprising that tall tales of hairy monsters haunt the world's highest mountain range, the Himalayas. Legend holds that across the towering mountaintops and icy crevices of the Himalayas walk the creatures that have terrified

WEIRD WORLD
IN 1961, THE GOVERNMENT OF NEPAL OFFICIALLY DECLARED THAT THE YETI EXISTS, MAKING IT THEIR NATIONAL SYMBOL AND EVEN USING ITS IMAGE ON THEIR STAMPS.

Tibetans for thousands of years – the Yeti. These savage beasts are known by several names. The people of Nepal call them "rakshasa", which means "demon", while their Tibetan name, "yeh-teh", translates to "that thing". Western journalists dubbed the creature The Abominable Snowman, a name they hoped would stir up fear – and sell more newspapers.

or of dark shapes seen scurrying across distant mountaintops, at speeds impossible for any human or known animal. However, no one has brought back positive evidence that the Yeti exists. Many people believe that the climbers actually saw some kind of large bear or ape, or simply needed to clean their snow goggles.

WEIRD WORLD

IN 1953, SIR EDMUND HILLARY AND HIS SHERPA PARTNER TENZING NORGAY FOUND GIANT FOOTPRINTS DURING THEIR RECORD-BREAKING ASCENT OF MOUNT EVEREST.

At 2 m (6 ft) tall, with a cone-shaped pointy head, a wide, toothy grin, hairy hunched shoulders, a stocky body, and shaggy arms stretching all the way to its knees, the beast is so strong it can toss chunks of frozen rock around like ice cubes. Its vocal range extends from high-pitched whistling to a lion-like roar, and the Yeti is said to like strong (alcoholic) drinks.

Over the years, many who climbed the peaks of Mount Everest in the Himalayas returned with tales of giant footprints in the ice and snow,

Big mountains, big monsters
In other parts of Asia these hairy creatures definitely live in the folklore of the people. The Almases, for example, are said to inhabit the Caucasus Mountains of Mongolia. Described as gentle and rather shy, these creatures are covered in reddish-brown fur, with thick "unibrows" hanging over their eyes and sticking-out jaws. Legends tell of many peaceful encounters between the Almases and humans. Some

SCIENTISTS ARE STILL SCRATCHING THEIR HEADS OVER WHETHER OR NOT THIS YETI SCALP FOUND IN TIBET IS A HOAX.

claim that Almases worked out a simple sign language so that they could communicate with people, and even do a little trading with them.

Rip-roaring tale

Hairy hominids also make themselves at home in European folklore and legend. The famous epic poem *Beowulf*, written in Old English, or Anglo Saxon, tells of a meeting between its hero, Beowulf, and a hairy human-like monster called Grendel.

A large, savage, hulking brute, Grendel made regular night-time visits to the Danish king's house for an unusual midnight snack – one or two sleeping guardsmen. One night, Beowulf lay in wait for Grendel, and while the creature paused between bites, Beowulf grabbed the shaggy beast. After an almighty wrestling match, Beowulf tore off one of Grendel's hairy arms with his bare hands. The enraged monster ran back to its cave, and the victorious Beowulf nailed the dismembered arm to the wall of the king's hall.

A HUGE AND HAIRY MONSTER IS JUST A SHORT STALK AWAY FROM AN UNSUSPECTING MOUNTAIN CLIMBER.

negative energy, accompanied by high-pitched humming and dark blobs covering the sky. Under the influence of this monstrous presence, climbers might be drawn towards a dangerous precipice, or feel so scared that they run blindly over the edge. If they're strong enough to resist, they run back down the mountain.

Bigfoot

Perhaps the most famous hairy humanoid of all is the North American beast we call Bigfoot, who is said to inhabit the dense forests of the Pacific Northwest. This creature is also known by its Native American name, Sasquatch, which translates to "hairy giant". Some tribal stories tell that Sasquatch began life as a human, but became an outcast whose hatred for other people twisted something inside him – as well as his appearance. And twisted it certainly is.

The towering terror stands as tall as a one-storey house, and weighs almost a tonne. It has five thick toes on its huge feet, and gives off an evil smell, somewhere between burning tyres and the stinky spray of a skunk or possum. If its smell

MacNightmare

Scotland has its own hairy, scary creature, who goes by the name of Fear Liath More, also known as the Big Grey Man. This beast has been encountered by lone climbers on Ben MacDhui in the Cairngorm Mountains.

Its appearance is remarkable enough (giant sized, with extremely long, waving arms, and occasionally wearing a top hat!), but the creature is especially scary because of its evil presence. Climbers may never see the beast, but instead they feel a terrible wave of

LOG ON!
For mo...
www.b...gfoot
...et

doesn't stop you in your tracks, its terrifying wails, shrieks, and bellows certainly will.

In many Native American legends, Bigfoots really do act like monsters. They kidnap humans (sometimes to eat, and other times – gulp – to breed with them). They viciously murder anyone who crosses their path. They rain boulders and uprooted trees down on campsites, while howling at all hours of the night. Some stories even tell of the creatures carrying walking sticks made of human shinbones.

Gentle giant

Bigfoot is said to have its gentle side as well. In one Native American legend, a fisherman meets Bigfoot near a lake and offers to share his catch with the starving creature. A few weeks later, he is surprised to find a pile of deerskins outside his home. The gifts keep coming and then there are no more. The fisherman thinks Bigfoot has moved away.

Years later, the same man encounters a rattlesnake in the forest, and passes out when it sinks its deadly fangs into him. When he comes around, he is being carried to his home by four Bigfoots, who have removed the rattlesnake venom and gently bandaged his wound. In this story, at least, the debt of the hairy monster has been repaid, once and for all.

A SEQUENCE OF STILL PHOTOGRAPHS FROM A CONTROVERSIAL 1967 AMATEUR FILM CAPTURE BIGFOOT ON THE MOVE.

CLASSIC MONSTERS

I n most ancient myths, monsters play a supporting role to the heroes. But in recent times, spine-chilling tales of more intelligent monsters have crept in, and now they get top billing. These are the classic monsters – of Frankenstein and Dracula – conjured up and brought to life in horror films. They have gripped our imaginations and become the baddies we love to fear.

AN ACTOR DRESSED AS FRANKENSTEIN'S MONSTER COMES COMPLETE WITH A ROW OF BOLTS TO KEEP HIS HEAD TOGETHER.

Man-made monster

It's unlikely that you'll ever open a cookery book and find a recipe for making a man. But scientists have long been fascinated by the possibility of bringing the dead back to life. By the 1800s, they had developed all sorts of tricks to revive people, including a whiff of smelling salts, a "kiss of life" to get breathing started again, even a jolt of electricity to wake up the nervous system. These well-publicized attempts to blur the boundaries between life and death helped inspire an English teenager to create one of the most terrifying creatures ever invented.

Frankenstein's monster

In the summer of 1816, the 19-year-old English author Mary Shelley and her husband, the poet Percy Shelley, went to Switzerland as guests of another poet, Lord Byron. Stuck indoors for much of the time, the guests entertained themselves with ghost stories and other scary fare. One day, they challenged each other to a writing contest to see who could conjure up the most horrifying tale. All those days of talking about graveyards, creepy castles, and strange goings-on in laboratories spilled over into Mary's nights. She began to have vivid dreams about reviving the dead, and putting together a creature from body parts. She used her nightmares as the basis for the classic horror novel, which she called *Frankenstein*.

What the doctor ordered

Mary's novel tells the story of a young medical student, Victor Frankenstein, who becomes obsessed with "reanimating" the dead. After some of his smaller experiments work, the doctor undertakes the ultimate science project – assembling the body parts of the dead to make a creature, then bringing it back to life.

When the patched-together person opens its eyes, the doctor is completely horrified – his creation is extremely tall, with flowing black hair and thin black lips. Its shriveled, yellow skin is so pale that he can see the veins pulsing underneath. In short, he has created a monster. With an almighty yell, Dr Frankenstein rushes out of his laboratory. Meanwhile, the monster ambles into the nearby village, where everyone who sees him screams and runs away.

The monster then goes into hiding, teaches himself to read, and begins to understand just what he is and why people fear

IN THIS GRUESOME STILL FROM THE 1973 FILM, *FRANKENSTEIN AND THE MONSTER FROM HELL*, DAVID PROWSE PLAYS THE MONSTER.

him. Feeling really rejected, he vows to take revenge on his creator. Leaving behind a trail of death and destruction, the monster eventually tracks down Dr Frankenstein, who is already dead. The creature realizes that

his time is up as well, and he goes off to meet his doom.

Frank goes to Hollywood

When the twisted tale of Dr Frankenstein and his monster made it to Hollywood – the 1931 movie classic was one of the first-ever horror films – some changes were made. The make-up artists decided that a doctor trying to stuff a stolen brain into an old skull would need to cut the bones right across. As a result, the first movie monster had a flat, square head, with visible stitches on his forehead. A pair of bolts in his neck served as connection points for the jolt of electricity that helped revive him. His tall, lumbering body was wrapped in unlovely green skin. In later versions, make-up artists really went to town, giving the monster gruesome features and hair everywhere.

In Shelley's tale the monster has a sensitive side and kills for revenge, but in the movies he runs amok like a big bully because he has accidentally been given a criminal's brain.

A POSTER FROM THE 1931 MOVIE, *DR JEKYLL AND MR HYDE*, WHICH STARRED FREDERIC MARCH.

the man is a respectable member of society, but as Mr Hyde he is completely out of control. Eventually, Dr Jekyll realizes he must end Mr Hyde's violent rages by poisoning himself... and his other self.

Prescription for terror

An equally gruesome medical man-monster pair is found in Scots author Robert Louis Stevenson's horrifying novel, Dr Jekyll and Mr Hyde. Stevenson, too, wrote his book after a particularly nasty dream – and nightmarish it certainly is. In his 1885 tale, Stevenson tells of a respectable doctor named Dr Jekyll, whose life becomes strangely connected with the actions of a despicable man who is called Mr Hyde. After a string of violent crimes draws attention to the good doctor, it is revealed that he has created a special potion to separate his good side from his more evil urges. When he is Dr Jekyll,

Fancy a bite?

The vampire has been a pain in the neck for centuries. This creep is one of the undead – a monster who should have passed on, but still hangs around in the world of the living.

KEEP AWAY FROM MAGIC POTIONS. IN THE STORY OF JEKYLL AND HYDE, THE DOCTOR'S BREW REVEALED HIS INNER MONSTER.

A vampire stays "alive" by rising up from the grave at night to drink the blood of living creatures, sucked through its horrid, flesh-piercing fangs – a very anti-social habit.

The myth of the vampire is found in tales from all over the globe. The Inuit people of Canada have their own legendary vampire, a terrifying baddy named Adlet. But the true home of these bloodthirsty beasts is the Slavic nations of Eastern Europe. This is where

WEIRD WORLD
ACCORDING TO SLAVIC LEGENDS, EVEN FRUIT AND VEGETABLES, SUCH AS PUMPKINS AND WATERMELONS, COULD BECOME VAMPIRES IF BITTEN BY ONE.

there are a whole host of stories about vampires preying on innocent people at the stroke of midnight, batlike beasts flying into bedrooms, and some very sore throats.

A TRAPDOOR IN A THEATRE STAGE IS KNOWN AS A VAMPIRE

A HOME-MADE, VAMPIRE- REPELLING KIT WOULD INCLUDE A ROPE OF GARLIC, A MIRROR, AND A CRUCIFIX.

Special skills

According to ancient legends, there are several ways to become a vampire. A bite in the neck or a blood transfusion from an existing vampire will probably get you on the team (although some victims simply die). Other cultures believed that a child born under a terrible curse or a person who committed suicide or who dabbled in witchcraft might become a vampire.

Once created, a vampire was given some pretty amazing skills. It could change shape, taking on the form of a bat or other creature, or appear

as a swirling mist in the night air. A vampire could control the minds of its potential victims, as well as the elements. Vampires could also move about with incredible strength and speed, and their senses were said to be superhuman. If a vampire fell from a high place, it could right itself in an instant.

Vampire rules

But even vampires had to follow the rules. In many legends, they had to return to their graves at the break of dawn, because sunlight was fatal to them. Vampires were also unable to cross running water, look at themselves in a mirror, or come through a doorway without an invitation.

However, the main things to avoid were the symbol of the Christian cross, or crucifix, and garlic. Those fearful of a vampire always made sure they had these objects to hand.

IN CENTRAL AND SOUTH AMERICA THERE ARE THREE SPECIES OF VAMPIRE BATS. TO STAY ALIVE THEY NEED BLOOD, JUST LIKE THE VAMPIRES THEY'RE NAMED AFTER

To kill a vampire

There were just as many rules about killing vampires. You could expose the monster to sunlight until it spontaneously combusted, put a wooden stake through its heart, or hold a cross up to its face. A shiny crucifix was particularly effective, as the vampire would also see its reflection. If that didn't work, a splash of garlic-laced holy water or a swift beheading usually did the trick. Vampires were said to be especially vulnerable to fire, so carrying a box of matches was another good option.

Count Dracula

When you think of a vampire, no doubt the creature you picture in your imagination was inspired by the blood-soaked 1897 book *Dracula*, by the Irish

63

novelist Bram Stoker. Stoker's vampire was quite the elegant gentleman – tall, dark, and dressed all in black. The Count was strangely pale and rather cold to the touch, as you might expect from an undead person, with two fang-like teeth ready to puncture a nearby neck. He had the physical strength of 20 men and the mental powers to hypnotize his victims. Count Dracula was able to change shape at will, turning himself into a bat, a wolf, a fine mist, or a powdery dust. Unlike many other vampires, he was able to walk about during the day, although his supernatural powers were useless in the sunlight. Oddly enough ,he never cast a shadow.

Vlad the impaler

Dracula couldn't have been real...or was he? Scholars believe Stoker found his vampire's name when researching the foul exploits of a Romanian ruler named Prince Vlad. The prince lived among the alpine peaks and castle ruins of the Transylvanian Alps in the 1400s. Vlad's dad was called Dracul, meaning "devil", and Vlad was known as Dracula, or "son of devil". Vlad lived in an age of constant and brutal warfare. People were forever being buried alive, blinded by a red-hot poker, or dropped through a trap door onto a bed of nails. Vlad had his own speciality – impaling his enemies on long poles stuck into the ground, an agonizing and slow way to die. The sight of someone dangling in the air like a huge kebab was enough to scare away potential

AFTER MAKING A MEAL OF HIS VICTIM'S BLOOD, DRACULA TUCKS HIMSELF INTO HIS COFFIN, HIS APPETITE SATISFIED FOR ONE MORE NIGHT.

invaders. Vlad was also reported to enjoy dipping his bread into human blood.

A FILM STILL FROM *THE BOY WHO THOUGHT HE WAS A WEREWOLF* (1973) CAPTURES THE TERRIFYING MADNESS OF A CREATURE THAT IS HALF MAN, HALF WOLF.

B y the light of a full moon The werewolf is a shape-shifting mythological monster, whose murderous rampages still make cinema audiences howl. Its name is a cross between "wolf" and an old Saxon word for man, "wer". According to legend, all it takes is a full Moon to change these otherwise ordinary-looking people into ferocious wolves. And they have all the cunning and agility of these expert night hunters, as well as the bite. Once transformed, werewolves roam through the night, devouring anything, from young children to corpses. When a werewolf dies, it is changed back into a human. The only effective weapon against these beasts is an object made of silver, especially silver arrows or bullets.

There are werewolf tales throughout the world. However, in places where wolves are not found, it's the full Moon instead that transforms people into other animals, such as bears, lions or tigers. In one Japanese myth the man-beast is a ferocious badger. Modern werewolf myths may have their roots in Greek mythology. One of these ancient stories tells of Lycaon, a king who was notorious for his cruel behaviour. He tried to find favour with the gods by offering them the flesh of a young child. The furious gods turned him into a wolf, and that's when the horrific howling began.

All wrapped up
Another popular film monster is the mummy. Imagine being stalked by a huge, silent creature wrapped in smelly old bandages, its arms outstretched to pull you back into its eternal tomb. You would be screaming for your real mummy. Many ancient people prepared bodies for burial by making them into mummies, a process perfected by the Egyptians. All the internal fluids and organs were pulled out of the dead body, which was wrapped in linen bandages before being placed in the tomb. Of course, it's one thing to see a mummy in a museum, but quite another to imagine one on the loose, bandages flapping, which is why these old favourites have filmgoers wrapped around their fingers.

Most movie mummies don't thrill by their incredible speed (it's hard to run when you're wrapped in bandages). Instead, they send shivers down your spine with their determination to get what they're after... hopefully, it's not you.

LOG ON...
Visit this werewolf site:
www.werewolfpage.com

WEIRD WORLD
SUPERSTITIOUS PEOPLE THINK THAT THE *TITANIC* SANK BECAUSE ITS HOLD CONTAINED A CURSED MUMMY, BEING TRANSPORTED TO A MUSEUM IN AMERICA. SOME THOUGHT IT WAS THE MUMMY'S REVENGE ON THOSE WHO HAD OPENED ITS BOX.

AN EGYPTIAN MUMMY IN A MUSEUM IS ONLY HALF AS GRUESOME AS A MUMMY ON THE RUN IN A HORROR FILM.

BIG BAD BULLIES

Giants in mythology start at size large. They tower over most of the other mythological monsters, strutting their great strength in a grouchy fashion and letting it be known that they have a giant appetite for human flesh. Many giants are a little bit stupid, which gives their enemies a fair chance of outwitting them. There are tales of kindly giants and giantesses, but in general big bad bullies behave as if they got out of the wrong side of their enormous beds.

THE NORSE FROST GIANTS TRIED TO STEAL THE GODS' TREASURES

EVEN A SMALLISH GIANT, SUCH AS THE BIBLICAL BEAST NAMED GOLIATH, WAS ABOUT 3 M (10 FT) TALL.

First of the giants
Giants have roamed the pages of mythology from the earliest times. Many different cultures even believe that giants were the first race of people on Earth. In Norse mythology, for example, it was said that the world was created where fiery hot air met cold mist and ice. As the ice began to thaw, its drips and drops formed the first creature – a giant named Ymir.

There was no Mrs Ymir, but somehow the giant managed to create a family without her. One of his legs produced a son with his other leg, and one male and one female giant grew from his armpit. Some of the other water drops formed a magical cow, whose udders gushed with rivers of milk to feed the giants. The cow licked the remaining ice and, as she did so, she uncovered the first ever god, freeing him from his icy trap.

Creating the Earth

Of course, when gods meet giants, there's big trouble. Wary of the growing giant population, the gods murdered Ymir, unleashing a torrent of blood that drowned all but two of the other giants. They recycled Ymir's immense body to form the Earth. His skull formed the sky, his flesh made the land, the rest of his blood filled the rivers and seas, his bones became mountains, his teeth created rocks and boulders, his hair turned into trees, and clouds were made from his brain. Even the giant's massive eyebrows were put to good use, as a dividing wall between the gods and the surviving giants.

IN NORSE MYTHOLOGY, THE FIRST GIANT – YMIR – WAS FORMED FROM DRIPS OF MELTING ICE.

Clash of the Titans

Why stop at one giant when you can have ten or more? The Titans were a family of 12 giants from Greek mythology who ruled the Earth just after its creation. These giants were the children of Uranus (the sky) and Gaia (the earth

THE SUPREME GOD ZEUS IN THE ACT OF KILLING IN HIS HEROIC CLASH WITH ONE OF THE TITANS.

birth. Desperate to save her sixth son Zeus from this fate, Rhea tricked Cronus into swallowing a rock that she had dressed up in baby clothes. She then hid Zeus away on a remote island. When he became a man, Zeus forced his dad to cough up his siblings. Together they succeeded in defeating the Titans and banishing them to the underworld. Zeus then became the ruler of the universe.

mother). But Uranus was not exactly a typical dad. He couldn't stand the sight of his kids, perhaps fearing their immense size and strength, so he forced them to live in the depths of the Earth. Gaia asked her children to help put an end to his unfair treatment, but only her youngest son Cronus agreed to help. With a brutal whack from a sharpened sickle, Cronus cut off his father's testicles and threw them into the sea. Then he took charge of the Earth.

Cronus later married his sister, Rhea. But he didn't deserve a father's day card, either. Fearing that his children would try to steal his throne, he gobbled them up soon after

Big brutes

Some giants worth keeping an eye out for are the Cyclopes. These monsters, known for their single, round eyes, smack in the middle of their huge foreheads, appeared in many Greek myths. In earlier tales, the one-eyed giants were blacksmiths to the gods, forging wonderful metal goods, from tridents to magical helmets. In fact, when people back then heard a volcano rumble, they assumed it was the sound of the Cyclopes slaving away in their vast underground forge. When Zeus was in trouble, these handy hulks could pluck lightning bolts from the skies and toss them down upon his enemies.

LOG ON...
librarythinkquest.org/
J011001O/Titans/titans.htm

In later tales, the cave-dwelling Cyclopes were no longer favourites of the gods. Instead, they were portrayed as shepherds with a burning desire for human flesh. In a story from the Greek poet Homer's epic tale, *Odyssey*, the hero Odysseus and a few of his bravest men were trapped when a huge Cyclops rolled a stone over the exit of a cave they were exploring. The hideous Cyclops greedily devoured several of the crew, but Odysseus had a trick or two up his sleeve. He got the monster drunk, then told him that his (Odysseus') name was Nobody. Later, he stuck the beast in the eye with a red-hot poker. The blinded giant ran around in pain, screaming, "Nobody hurt me!" Of course, this got no response whatsoever, and our heroes managed to make their escape.

Girl power

A large number of female giants lived in ancient Ireland, among them Bedb, who was so tall she could put a foot on each side of a river. Another was named Eriu, the giantess that gave Ireland its name, Eire.

Another female giant – the horrible Harthgrepa of German legend – used magic to make herself smaller or larger, without even going on a diet.

In America, the woods of the Pacific Northwest are home to a particularly nasty giantess named Tsonoqwa. (If she invites you to dinner at

BEAUTY MEETS THE BEAST – IN THIS CASE, THE GIANT GREEN OGRE FROM THE FILM *SHREK*.

her place you'd be foolish to go, because you're on the menu.) Legend tells that she wanders the woods with a basket on her back for collecting children – to eat.

Perhaps the most fantastic female giant is the Norse Skadi, said to be able to lift a boat full of men in one hand. Skadi liked to crisscross the mountaintops on oversized skis, probably causing a spectacular avalanche or two.

ACCORDING TO LEGEND, PAUL BUNYAN CREATED AMERICA'S GRAND CANYON AS HE DRAGGED HIS HUGE AXE BEHIND HIM.

J ack the giant killer

Greedy, stupid giants stomp around in many fairy tales. The most famous of these ancient tales reveals exploits of a farm

A MASK OF THE WILD WOMAN OF THE WOODS, TSONOQWA, WHO ROASTED CHILDREN ON HOT ROCKS FOR HER TEA.

72

again he managed to slay the creature. One after another, Jack wiped out almost every type of giant you can imagine, earning the right to live happily after.

Gentle giant

Not all giants are monsters though. Meet Paul Bunyan, the giant North American lumberjack, whose tales were spun around the woodstove each night by loggers looking for a laugh. They say it took five storks working overtime to deliver the giant baby, and when he was only one week old he was already wearing his father's clothes.

boy from Cornwall named Jack. The first giant he managed to outwit was a 7 m (21 ft) terror with red hair and wild eyes, whose waist was so big it took ten minutes to circle him. Jack's next gigantic foe ate a bathtub full of porridge every morning. His third victim had two ugly heads. Luckily for Jack, there was not much inside them, and once

When Paul grew so large that he had to use wagon wheels for buttons, his family moved him out of the house and onto a raft in a nearby lake, where his smallest movement caused boat-tipping tides. Paul played with axes the way other kids play with toys, and when he grew up he became a lumberjack, working with a loyal crew of other big men. His best mate was Babe, a giant blue ox who was so big it took a bird a whole day to fly from one horn to the other. Paul and Babe walked all the way across North America, leaving a trail of wonderful tales (and some pretty big footprints) behind.

SCARY FAIRIES

I t's a myth that all fairies are good and kind. In fairy tales the world over, fairies and their relatives are held responsible for mischievous acts. These mini-monsters are a magical mix of helpful and harmful. Some are just plain scary. Good and bad fairies like nothing better than to surprise, tease, and play tricks on humans – sometimes even lead them astray or into grave danger.

THIS 1997 FILM *FAIRY TALE: A TRUE STORY* IS BASED ON THE CLAIM OF TWO ENGLISH GIRLS THAT THEY HAVE PHOTOS OF FAIRIES.

It's a small world

To get to know fairies, first you must find them. That's not always easy because some fairies, such as those in Shakespeare's *A Midsummer Night's Dream*, can make themselves invisible. Start by looking down – most fairies resemble humans, but are much smaller. Some are pretty, with gossamer wings, while others have shrivelled heads and

LOG ON...
www.faeries.
org/site/lore/faes.html

WEIRD WORLD

A CIRCULAR BAND OF GRASS IN A FIELD OR GARDEN IS CALLED A FAIRY RING. ALTHOUGH IT LOOKS LIKE A MINIATURE DISCO FOR FAIRY DANCING, IT IS IN FACT CAUSED BY MUSHROOM-LIKE FUNGI.

hunchbacks. You'll also need to sort your pixies (good spirits) from your nixes (nasty water elves), because the name a fairy goes by often depends on where it comes from.

Fairies are nature lovers, who make their homes inside hollow hills or trees, among leaves and flowers, or under waterfalls. Some live alone, while others live in Fairyland, an enchanted

traditional stories, or folk tales, some elves are extremely good beings who flit through the air, dance in the morning dew, or peek down at you from the treetops. Many of these small wonders treat humans with kindness and affection, helping out in many different ways.

Little elves called brownies, for example, have attractive dark eyes and nimble fingers. They are happy to pitch in with household tasks for the families they attach themselves to. Brownies are not visible to disbelieving adults, but good children are able to see them.

FAIRIES CAN MAKE THEMSELVES INVISIBLE WHENEVER THEY WANT

place ruled by a fairy king and queen.

Mini-beasts
One famous fairy creature from Norse and Celtic mythology is the elf, known for its pointy ears as well as its mischievous streak. According to

MAGIC MAKES SHAKESPEARE'S FAIRY QUEEN FALL IN LOVE WITH AN ASS.

THE ELF IS THE MOST HUMAN LOOKING OF ALL THE FAIRYFOLK. IN THIS SCENE FROM *THE LORD OF THE RINGS*, THE BRAVE ELF LEGOLAS GREENLEAF TAKES AIM.

The Heinzelmännchen (little men) of German folk tales are similar to brownies, and are also handy around the house.

Evil elves

Not all elves are handsome and helpful. Some like nothing better than to make trouble for people. In Norse mythology, bad elves known as Swartalfar were originally spawned from the maggots that feasted on the dead giant Ymir's flesh. These evil-doers lived deep under the earth and never came out into daylight, in case they were turned to stone.

The Scots people no doubt wished for a similar fate for Nuckelavee, the vilest elf imaginable. This beast is said to have a single, fire-rimmed eye, arms that reach its ankles, and a huge watermelon-sized head. The horrid creature has no skin. You can see the black blood pulsing through its veins, and its muscles and internal organs are also visible. Thankfully, this particular elf has a weakness – it's afraid of running water. All you have to do is jump across the nearest brook or stream to escape from the creature.

Sprightly sprites

Hopefully, you won't step on a sprite, an elf-like creature often found in watery places. A sprite's favourite pastime is to make mischief. Sometimes these are harmless pranks, like stealing food, hiding household objects, or knocking over a vase of flowers. Igosha, for example, is a sprite from Russian folklore, who has no hands, but plenty of tricks up its sleeve. The only way to stop Igosha from creating chaos in your home is to always set a place for it at the table.

Other sprites pull some pretty awful stunts too. The nixes, which are sprites from Norse mythology, are always trying to lure people into the water, and to their deaths. Luckily, nixes are easy to spot because the hems of their clothes are always soaking wet.

Irish legends tell of a magical little sprite called the leprechaun.

These merry men, often shown wearing old-fashioned shoes with buckles and a cobbler's apron, make shoes for other fairy folk during the day. At night, they like to throw wild parties that sometimes end with moonlit rides on the back of the family dog. Many people believe that leprechauns guard a pot of gold, which is up for grabs – if you can grab the leprechaun first.

IF LUCK IS WITH YOU, YOU'LL OUTWIT THIS WILY LEPRECHAUN AND GRAB HIS STASH OF GOLD.

Gobbling goblins

The little people elves can never see eye-to-eye with are goblins. These squat, often ugly little critters live among tree roots and moss-covered rock clefts. It is said that a goblin's smile is enough to curdle blood, while its laughter could instantly sour milk. Like sprites, goblins get their kicks from tricks. Apart from the usual switching round of signposts and other playful antics, a goblin's games can harm people, if not kill them.

Mara, a Scandinavian goblin, likes snatching people from their beds at night and taking away their ability to walk and talk. Erlking, a goblin from German folklore, lures unwary travellers, especially children, into the deepest woods to meet their deaths.

A slightly less evil branch of the goblin family is a group of misshapen little people called gnomes. They live under the earth, keeping a close watch on its treasures.

Little legends

Dwarves are little folk about half the size of a human, with stocky, hairy bodies and long beards – even on the females.

Dwarves generally make their homes in underground caves. These little gems often work down the mines in folk legend, loading up their tiny swag bags with all manner of mineral riches.

Dwarves have a reputation throughout mythology for their craftsmanship. The objects they make – from magical rings to mighty hammers – often have special powers. The Norse dwarf Alvis forged weapons for the gods that made them invincible in battle, while Dvalin the dwarf from German tales wove wigs of pure gold.

Terrible trolls

If you ever visit Fairyland, you must avoid trolls at all costs. If

WITH HIS TWISTED FEATURES, THE EVIL GOBLIN IS ONE OF THE UGLIEST OF THE FAIRY FOLK, AS SEEN IN THE FILM *LEGEND*.

not, you might pay with your life. These cave dwellers have scaly greyish-green skin, huge, bulbous noses and knuckles that

flowing hair and red-rimmed eyes, always awash with tears. It is said that a banshee makes her home near a family, and when someone in this "adopted" family is about to die, she lets out a horrible wail and a fresh flood of tears. In the Scots version of this tale, the banshee is said to wail while washing the clothes of the doomed person.

scrape the cave floor. Occasionally, they sprout repulsive tusks. But it's not just their looks that kill. These beasts have an insatiable desire for human flesh, coupled with immense strength that makes resistance futile. The best thing to do is hold out until sunrise. Like many fairy creatures, the tiniest sliver of sunlight is enough to make these beasts burst.

The bogeyman (known in some places as bugaboo) is an evil spirit or goblin who crops up in African myths. He is the ultimate bad fairy, who kidnaps disobedient children – or so the story was told to naughty boys and girls 100 or so years ago.

Banshees and bogeymen
There are several bad-news bearers in Fairyland. In Irish folk legend, female fairies called banshees have long,

WEIRD WORLD
AN ANCIENT PREVENTION TECHNIQUE FOR KEEPING BAD FAIRIES AWAY WAS TO SPRINKLE YOURSELF WITH A FEW FLAKES OF PORRIDGE OATS, OR PUT SOME IN YOUR POCKET.

WICKED WITCHES

With a bubbling cauldron full of bats and toads, most wicked witches can stir up trouble wherever they go. They are the undisputed experts of magic in mythology, and they have the power to make something happen or change, for better or worse. Sometimes witches cast magic spells to bring good luck, but in most tales they are definitely up to no good.

The power of witchcraft

We often think of witches as crinkly crones with hooked noses, rotten teeth and a chinful of warts. Wizards are depicted as white-haired men with piercing eyes and flowing robes. In mythology, however, many witches and wizards look just like everyone else. It's their secret knowledge that sets them apart.

The art of using magic (whether naughty or nice) to affect people or change the course of events is called witchcraft. People have believed in its power since ancient times, using special witchy tricks to help ensure a successful hunt or a bumper harvest. In many cultures, people regard those who master the art of witchcraft as wise and wonderful, able to help and heal. Others see witchcraft as something more sinister, barely a broomstick's length away from evil.

WITCHES DO THEIR MAGIC AT MIDNIGHT, THE WITCHING TIME

Which witch?

Magic-makers in mythology go by all sorts of names, from sorceress to shaman.

TYPICAL IMAGES OF WITCHES FEATURE A POINTY CHIN, HOOKED NOSE, AND A TALL BLACK HAT. THEY TRAVEL ON A BROOMSTICK ACCOMPANIED BY A BLACK CAT.

LOG ON...
www.angelfire.com/
tx5/worldofmagic/faq.html

The most common name, witch, has its roots in an old German word that means to bend or turn (as witches try to twist things with magic). A witch is usually female, although there are also male witches, sometimes called warlocks, wizards, or sorcerers. Some witches and wizards inherit their powers from their parents, while others go to special schools (like the fictional Harry Potter), where they learn supernatural powers from skilled sorcerers.

S ky high

One of the wickedest witch skills is the ability to fly. Many witches can zoom about by themselves, while others hitch a lift on a broom, garden tools such as hoes and spades, or a magical flying animal. One weird witch from Russian

WEIRD WORLD

A MONSTROUS WITCH FROM PHILIPPINE LEGEND SPLITS HERSELF IN TWO WHENEVER THERE IS A FULL MOON. HER TOP HALF SPROUTS WINGS, ENABLING HER TO FLY, WHILE HER LOWER HALF JUST SITS AROUND.

81

WITCHES AND WIZARDS CLAIM THAT MAGIC GIVES THEM MYSTERIOUS POWERS. SOME USE IT TO UNLOCK PAST SECRETS, WHILE OTHERS BELIEVE THEY CAN SEE INTO THE FUTURE.

WEIRD WORLD
IN MEDIEVAL EUROPE, MANY CATS WERE WIPED OUT IN MASSACRES, AS SOME PEOPLE WERE CONVINCED THAT ALL CATS WERE IN CAHOOTS WITH WITCHES. EVEN TODAY, SUPERSTITION LINGERS WHEN A BLACK CAT CROSSES YOUR PATH.

legend, Baba Yaga, zips through the skies on a kitchen implement – the mortar and pestle. When she doesn't get her way, she goes ballistic – and cannibalistic, threatening to eat anyone who defies her.

Shape-shifters

You would definitely sit up and take notice if a witch on a broomstick zoomed overhead, but an owl could pass by without attracting much attention. This is why many witches rely on shape-shifting, the ability to temporarily morph themselves into an animal so that they can go about their work in secret.

AT HOGWARTS SCHOOL, APPRENTICE WIZARD HARRY POTTER IS TAUGHT HOW TO CAST SPELLS AND USE MAGIC FOR GOOD, TO OVERCOME EVIL.

Many witches are assisted by "familiars". These are spirits who often take the forms of familiar animals such as cats (particularly black ones), toads, snakes, mice, or owls. Most witches choose to take the shape of their familiars, but there are some wild exceptions, from leopards in African legend to hyenas in ancient Egypt.

The Finnish witch Louhi can turn herself into an eagle with a hundred swordsmen under her wings and a thousand archers on her tail. And there are the Navajo skinwalkers, Native American witches so scary that their name must never be spoken. They transform themselves into wolves, bears, or coyotes and take on the traits of each animal – for example, strength or cunning – to carry out their evil deeds.

Spellbound

Another sorcerer's skill is casting spells. A spell is like a recipe for a particular act of magic and can be short and sweet or long and involved. The instructions for casting a spell might include repeating magic words, performing special moves, or mixing up a powder or potion to create a change in someone. To assist

FROM THE 15TH TO THE 18TH CENTURY PEOPLE WERE TRIED IN COURT IF THEY WERE SUSPECTED OF PRACTISING WITCHCRAFT.

with this ritual, a witch has a toolkit of "magic" objects, from wands and brooms to cauldrons and chalices. There are good spells that heal and protect, and others that bring money or love. Evil spells – hexes and curses – are by far the most popular in mythology.

Mad magic

One caster of spells who got completely out of hand was Medea, a legendary magic-maker of Ancient Greece and the wife of one of its heroes, Jason. She didn't always use her witchcraft for evil, but when Jason left her for another woman, the scorned sorceress went completely mad. She gave his new bride a poisoned crown and wedding dress that burned her (and her poor father, who tried to rescue her) to a crisp. Then she got out of town fast, on a chariot pulled by dragons.

Death witch

Many evil witches in mythology are closely linked with death. Hecate, a three-headed witch of Ancient Greece could be found at a crossroads at night. One of her heads resembled a dog, one a snake, and the other a horse. Each head faced in a different direction, allowing her to see anyone coming her way. People were so scared of her that they sacrificed lambs and puppies just to keep her happy.

A powerful symbol of death and magic in Russia is the wizard Koshchei the Deathless. He is named "deathless" because his soul is hidden inside an egg, inside a duck, inside a rabbit, which is locked in a chest and buried under a tree on an island far out to sea. Koshchei travels about on an all-seeing horse, in search of maidens to abduct. One victim, Marena, uncovers his secret and spills the beans to a hero, who finds the egg and nearly brings death to Deathless. In this myth, at least, the monster manages to re-invent himself for more magical mayhem.

REFERENCE SECTION

Whether you've finished reading *Myths and Monsters*, or are turning to this section first, you'll find the information on the next eight pages really useful. Here is the mythology timeline, a gruesome glossary, some monstrous hoaxes, and a guide to sacred places. You'll also find a list of website addresses – so whether you want to surf the net or search out extra facts, these pages should turn you from a monster fan into an expert.

MYTHS AND MONSTERS TIMELINE

c.40,000 BC
The first inhabitants of Australia, the Aboriginal people, begin to recite and sing the sacred stories of their origins. Together with special rituals, they are known as The Dreaming, or Dreamtime.

c.30,000 BC
The early people of Africa paint images on the walls of caves, probably related to the mythology of their varied culture.

c.10,000 BC
Inuit people of North America record images from their mythology by painting them on sealskins.

c.5000 BC
The Sumerians, who lived in what is now southern Iraq, develop a rich mythology. By 3500 BC they have created a form of writing called cuneiform. Later, they will use cuneiform to record their stories of gods and heroes.

3100 BC
The Egyptian king joins Upper and Lower Egypt into one land. The newly united people begin collecting and ordering their myths, using hieroglyphs (the picture writing system that developed at about the same time). Some hieroglyphs illustrate stories of Egyptian gods.

2000 BC
The Mesopotamian Empire, which flourishes in the Persian Gulf, has a lively mythology of gods. At about the same time, the Shang dynasty emerges in China. The Chinese people worship their king's ancestors as gods.

1500 BC
India develops a system of gods, handing down their stories in special hymn collections called Vedas. The first of these Vedas was probably written down in 900 BC.

1400–1200 BC
The Mycenaean people, who lived in present-day Greece, make sculptures of their gods.

700 BC
Three poetry collections – the *Theogony* by Hesiod, and the *Iliad* and the *Odyssey* by Homer – record the mythology of Greece, introducing its major characters and themes. At about this time, the Romans come into contact with the Greeks, and some of the characteristics and actions of Greek gods and heroes start to appear in Roman myths.

500 BC
Celtic people settle in the British Isles, especially Ireland. They bring with them an ancient oral (speaking) tradition of myth cycles, or collections. Later, Irish monks collect and write down these cycles.

200 BC
The Roman poet Virgil writes an epic poem called the *Aeneid*, which links Greek and Roman mythology.

c.1000 AD
The only surviving manuscript of the epic poem *Beowulf* is from this time, although it was first transcribed (written down) by an anonymous author in the 8th century. Long before it is written down, the poem is recited or sung.

1200
A collection of Norse mythology called the *Eddas* is written down. It contains tales of gods and heroes.

1300
The Aztecs of central Mexico create a complicated mythology, featuring gods of earlier civilizations as well as gods of people they have conquered. On Easter Island, mysterious statues of huge heads are erected.

1403-09
The world's first encyclopedia and its longest work of nonfiction, the *Yongle Dadian*, is compiled in China. It contains some mythology.

1818
Mary Shelley publishes her monster hit book *Frankenstein* in London.

1855
Thomas Bulfinch publishes his mythology collection, *The Age of Fable* (later known as *Bulfinch's Mythology*).

1886
Robert Louis Stevenson publishes his novel *The Strange Case of Dr Jekyll and Mr Hyde*.

1897
Bram Stoker publishes the classic vampire tale, *Dracula*.

1920
Legendary actor John Barrymore brings the story of Dr Jekyll and Mr Hyde to life on film.

1921
A newspaper columnist describes the Yeti as an "Abominable Snowman" for the first time.

1922
The silent film of the vampire tale *Nosferatu* is shown in cinemas.

1931
Boris Karloff stars in the horror film classic of Mary Shelley's *Frankenstein*.

1954
The 3-D film *The Creature from the Black Lagoon* hits cinema screens.

1963
In a film version of *Jason and the Argonauts*, the legendary hero battles monsters from mythology.

1967
Two amateur filmmakers capture Bigfoot on film near Bluff Creek, California. It's still not known if the film is real or a hoax.

1971
Sonar is used to look for Nessie in the waters of Loch Ness, Scotland

1981
The film *American Werewolf in London* combines humour and horror.

1992
A modern cinema version of Bram Stoker's *Dracula* is shown.

1993
Anne Rice publishes the first title of her successful vampire chronicles, *Interview with a Vampire*.

1995
A leopard's skull, thought to be part of the Beast of Bodmin Moor, is found in Cornwall, England.

1998
J. K. Rowling's *Harry Potter and the Philosopher's Stone* is published.

1999
The blockbuster film *The Mummy* unwraps the horror of this monster.

2001
The fun film *Monsters Inc* is released in the UK and is a big hit. The same year, Dreamworks SKG makes the film *Shrek*, about a bad giant who turns good. On 19 December a film version of the first part of Tolkien's *Lord of the Rings* premieres around the world.

GRUESOME GLOSSARY

Aquatic
Living or growing in water.

Camouflage
Special markings or colours that allow animals to blend in with their surroundings.

Cannibal
A person who eats human beings.

Curse
An appeal to a supernatural power to bring harm to someone.

Dismember
Removing the arms and legs of a person or animal.

Familiar
A supernatural spirit, usually an animal, that assists a witch or wizard.

Fiend
An evil spirit or very wicked person.

Flipper
A flat, oar-shaped limb of an aquatic animal, used for swimming.

Giant
A mythical person of superhuman size and strength.

God
In mythology, a supernatural being who rules some part of the world, or represents one of Earth's forces.

Goddess
A female god.

Hero
In mythology, a person of incredible strength and courage who wins respect for their actions.

Impale
To pierce with a very sharp object.

Labyrinth
A maze-like network of passages.

Legend
A popular story handed down through generations, but not generally regarded as true.

Magic
The art of controlling natural forces.

Medieval
Of the Middle Ages, the period between about AD 500 and 1500.

Mermaid
An imaginary creature with the head and upper body of a woman and the tail of a fish.

Monster
An imaginary beast that is abnormal or unnatural in some way.

Myth
A story, often about superhuman beings, which early people used to explain natural events or things they didn't understand. Myths were generally regarded as true.

Mythology
A collection of myths, especially those from a particular culture.

Nectar
In mythology, the drink of the gods.

Prophecy
A prediction or a guess.

Ritual
A set of rules, or a procedure, that is the same every time.

Sacrifice
Killing a person or animal to please a god.

Saurian
Looking like a lizard.

Shaman
Religious leader, who is also a healer among some Native American tribes.

Shape-shift
The ability to change into another shape or form, and back again.

Sorcerer
A person who uses magic powers.
Spell
A formula that has magical power.
Superhuman
Having powers that are above and beyond those of ordinary people.
Supernatural
Not explained by science or logic.
Tentacle
An animal's long, flexible organ.
Undead
In mythology, a corpse that is brought to life, for example, a zombie, vampire, or mummy.

Underworld
In mythology, the home of the dead, underneath the Earth.
Vampire
An undead person who rises from the grave each night to feast on the blood of living creatures.
Venom
Poison liquid produced by animals and usually passed on through a bite.
Witch
A person who practises magic.
Witchcraft
The art of using magic or controlling supernatural forces.

NAME YOUR MONSTER

Monsters and mythical creatures go by many names, depending on where they're from. If you want to name them all, use this list of aliases.

Bigfoot
Sasquatch (Canada); Yahoo, Yowie (Australia); Almas (Russia).
Dragon
Amphiptere, drake, firedrake, lindworm, wyrm, wyvern; drakon (Greece); draco (Latin); long (China); draak (Dutch); smok (Poland).
Fairy
Fee, fay, faerie, green children, pixie, changeling, little people, brownies, bogies, hobgoblins, elf; verry volk (Wales); nix, kobold (Germany).
Mermaid
Merrymaid, merrow; ningyo (Japan); aino (Finland); kaala (Hawaii); lorelei, melusine (Germany); rusalka

(Russia); aspara (India).
Unicorn
Ki-lin (China); kirin (Japan).
Werewolf
Limikkin (Native America); wendigo (Canada); nahaul (Mexico); Lang Ren (China); vrykolaka (Greece).
Witch
Warlock, wizard, weird sister, hag, crone, bogglebo, sorcerer, sorceress, enchantress, mystic, seer, shaman, witch doctor; Wihunga (Native America); Wu (China).
Vampire
Vampyre; nosferatu (Romania); eretica (Russia); rakshasa (India); doppelsauger (Germany); kuang-shi (China); langsuir (Malaysia); jaracacas (Brazil); kasha (Japan).
Yeti
Abominable Snowman, Kachenjunga demon; rakshasa (Nepal); Dzu-teh, Teh-lma, Mi-teh (Tibet).

MONSTROUS HOAXES

Many of the wildest tales about so-called monsters come from someone's imagination, with no real-life evidence. Sometimes, these are hoaxes or pranks, designed to fool as many people as possible. Often, they are simply cases of mistaken identity.

Beast of Gevudan
Gevudan, France, 1760s
In the mountains of south-central France in 1764 a ferocious, wolf-like creature killed as many as 60 men, women, and children. The king sent troops to the region, and in 1767 the creature was shot and killed. In case it turned out to be a werewolf, the hunter used silver bullets. The beast's remains were paraded through the streets before being buried in a secret location. In 1997, a man working in a Paris museum studied the surgeons' reports from the time. He concluded that the beast was a striped hyena.

Feejee Mermaid
New York City, New York 1842
A mysterious English doctor arrived in New York in 1842 with the preserved body of a mermaid. He claimed he had bought the creature in South America. When circus manager P.T. Barnum stepped in to promote the doctor's mermaid "show" across the nation, his posters of a beautiful female mermaid drew huge crowds. Of course, the "doctor" was a friend of Barnum's, hired to act the part, and his "mermaid" was a dead monkey sewn to a fish. The only thing that was real was the fortune Barnum made from his hoax.

Cottingley Fairies
West Yorkshire, England 1917
When nine-year-old Frances Griffiths and her cousin borrowed a camera to take photographs of fairies, no one paid much attention. But, when the pictures were developed, Frances appeared to be surrounded by tiny fairy folk. The amazing photos were seen by Sir Arthur Conan Doyle (the creator of Sherlock Holmes), who published them, together with an article claiming that fairies exist. Experts said the photos were genuine, and many people accepted it. However, in the 1980s, Frances told an interviewer that the photos were a hoax. The fairies were paper cutouts held in the ground with hatpins.

Caddy, the Cadboro Bay Serpent
British Columbia, Canada, 1937
Cadboro Bay's most famous resident, the long-necked sea serpent nicknamed Caddy, has astonished onlookers for centuries. Hundreds of eyewitness reports tell of a long, hump-backed beast with flippers and a split tail, ripping around the bay at top speed. In 1937, what was believed to be the carcass of Caddy was pulled from the stomach of a dead whale. This incredible find was described as 3 m (10 ft) long, with skin like a snake and a horse-shaped head. It was later revealed to be that of a premature baby whale.

SACRED PLACES

A few places around the world are considered to be sacred, or have special importance in mythology.

Devil's Tower

This massive, stump-shaped rock, a sacred site to many Native American tribes, rises 365 m (1,200 ft) over the American state of Wyoming.

Easter Island

A speck of land in the South Pacific, between Tahiti and Chile, Easter Island was the ancient home of the Rapa Nui. More than 300 huge stone statues, called Moai, are dotted along the coastline. The Moai were erected about AD 1500, perhaps to represent the spirits of their leaders, or to communicate with the gods.

Great Pyramid of Giza

The Great Pyramid at Giza (near Cairo, Egypt) is the oldest, and only, survivor of the seven wonders of the ancient world. Built about 2500 BC, the pyramid took 20 years to assemble. The pyramid is mostly solid, but passages inside lead to special chambers that house the tomb of a dead king (Khufu).

Loch Ness

Loch Ness in Scotland, the legendary home of the serpent monster, Nessie, is the third largest lake in Europe. It was formed during the last Ice Age, and the volcanic tremors that helped to create its scar-like shape still rumble through the region.

Mt Fuji

This beautiful mountain, a dormant (not currently active) volcano near Tokyo, Japan, is an important national symbol as well as a sacred place. Japanese legends say that the mountain rose all at once from a flat plain in about 300 BC, but geographers say that Fuji is much older than this.

Mt Olympus

A rugged mountain in northern Greece, Mt Olympus was believed to be the heavenly home of the Greek gods and the site of Zeus' throne. The exact location of the mountain is not pinpointed in mythology, but experts think that it is most likely to be Olympus.

Stonehenge

This gigantic rock circle at Stonehenge in southwest England might have been built as a temple, an observatory, or a sacred burial ground. The huge, flat stones, which align with the Sun, Moon, and stars, were laid in about 2500–1500 BC.

Uluru

Also known as Ayers Rock, this huge sandstone outcrop rises from the deserts of central Australia. It seems to change colour as the Sun moves across the desert, from bluish purple to fiery orange. In the nooks and caves of the rock, Aboriginal paintings, thousands of years old, show how sacred Uluru is to the original people of Australia.

MYTHS AND MONSTERS WEBSITES

General sites
www.bulfinch.org
The online version of this classic collection of myths.

www.pibburns.com/myth.htm
This site explores myth and legend – from ancient times to the space age.

www.themystica.org
One website, two online encyclopedias – myth and folklore, and magic and the paranormal.

www.legends.dm.net
Folklore as seen through the eyes of some of its major characters.

http://webhome.idirect.com/~donlong/monsters/monsters.htm
An encyclopedia of monsters and mythical creatures.

http://members.bellatlantic.net/~vze33gpz/myth.html
A huge collection of mythology reference materials and links.

www.mythinglinks.org
A fantastic illustrated collection of links to the mythologies of the world.

www.clubi.ie/lestat/godsmen.html
Of Gods and Men – an invaluable mythology reference.

www.probertencyclopaedia.com/mythology.htm
A who's who (and what's what) of world mythology.

www.unmuseum.org/unmain.htm
The Museum of Unnatural Mystery – a very cool place to explore some puzzling monster mysteries.

www.monstrous.com
A massive site covering monsters, from mythology to the movies.

www.mythweb.com
A great site devoted to the heroes, gods, and monsters of Greek mythology, with cool graphics.

http://library.thinkquest.org/12865/mray/bobcave.htm
Click anywhere on this unique world map to explore myths and legends from that particular region.

www.windows.ucar.edu/cgi-bin/tour.cgi?link=/mythology/mythology.html
A site chock-full of examples of how cultures used myths to explain the physical world.

Other sites

http://bestiarium.net/index-e.html
The Dragon Bestiary, a field guide to dragons throughout history.

www.polenth.demon.co.uk/
The Dragon Stone – a guide to dragons, ancient and modern.

www.lone-star.net/literature/beowulf/
Read and study the monstrous epic poem right here.

http://theshadowlands.net/serpent.htm
Learn more about the world's sea serpents and lake monsters.

www.lochness.co.uk
Check out the live Loch Ness webcam.

www.nessie.co.uk
Nessie's official home page on the Internet.

www.bigfootcentral.com
All about Bigfoot and its sightings, including a few fun games.

www.yowiehunters.com
Everything you need to know about the Australian monster, Yowie.

www.vampires.com
You'll be up to your neck in vampire lore if you check out this site.

www.draculascastle.com
Take a virtual tour of Vlad the Impaler's Romanian castle.

http://rhs.jack.k12.wv.us/classic/welcome.htm
Loads of cool pics from some of the greatest monster movies of all time.

http://thefae.freeservers.com
Step inside the magical realm of fairy creatures on this site.

http://home-1.worldonline.nl~hamberg/
Take a look at Mary Shelley's *Frankenstein*.

www.monsterhunters.org
A site dedicated to exploration of Loch Ness in the quest to find Nessie.

www.cryptozoology.com
A site dedicated to the world's mystery animals, from Sasquatch to Nessie.

www.mythandmystery.com
A huge collection of links to the world's myths and mysteries.

www.forteanpix.demon.co.uk
A bizarre photo gallery of some of the monsters in this book.

www.museumofhoaxes.com
Take a look at these monster hoaxes and see if you've been taken in.

INDEX

CREDITS

Dorling Kindersley would like to thank:
Chris Bernstein for the index.

Additional photography:
Frank Greenaway, Dave King, Alex Wilson and Jerry Young.

Picture Credits

The publishers would like to thank the following for their kind permission to reproduce their photographs:
Position key: a = above; b = bottom; c = centre; l = left; r = right; t = top

3: Ronald Grant Archive c; 4: Corbis: Frank Lane Picture Agency tl; 5: Ronald Grant Archive b; 7: Corbis/Carl and Ann Purcell br; 8: Ronald Grant Archive; 9: Bridgeman Art Library, London/New York; Bibliotheque Nationale, Paris, France. Archives Charmet tl; 10-11: Corbis/Nathan Benn; 11: Werner Forman Archive/Private Collection, London bl; 12: Ancient Art & Architecture Collection tr; 13: Bridgeman Art Library, London/New York, Vatican Museums and Galleries, Vatican City, Italy/Giraudon/Lauros b; 14: Ronald Grant Archive b; 14-15: Kobal Collection, Disney/Pixar t; 17: Mary Evans Picture Library br; 18-19: Masterfile UK r; Ian Lloyd b; 19: Danish National Museum tr; 20: British Museum br; The Natural History Museum, London tl; 21: Bridgeman Art Library, London/New York, National Gallery, London b; 22: Corbis/Vanni Archives t; 23: RSPCA/Adrian Warren/Wild Images b; 24: Corbis/Bettmann br; 25: Corbis/Jeffrey L. Rotman br; 26: Corbis/Bettmann t; Bridgeman Art Library, London/New York, Bargello, Florence, Italy; 28: Bridgeman Art Library, London/New York, Royal Library, Copenhagen tl; 28-9: Corbis/Ralph White c; 29: Fortean Picture Library/Anthony Shiels cr; 30: Werner Forman Archive/Museum of Anthropology, University of British Columbia, Vancouver br; 32: Corbis/Frank Lane Picture Agency; 32-33: N.A.S.A t; 33: Mary Evans Picture Library/Brenda Hartill br; 35: N.H.P.A./Morten Strange tl; 36-37: Corbis/Ralph A. Clevenger; 37: Corbis/Ralph A. Clevenger c; 38: Michael Holford/Museum of Mankind; 39: Corbis/Jeff Vanuga b; The Art Archive/Museum fur Volkerkunde Vienna/Dagli Orti cr; 40: Fortean Picture Library/Dorothy Hartley tl; 41: Museum of Mankind b; Hamburgisches Museum Für Völkerkunde c; 44 Tony Souter background; 46: The Natural History Museum, London; 47: Fortean Picture Library; 48: Corbis/Eric Crichton b; 48-49: AKG London/Erich Lessing; 49: Corbis/Angelo Hornak br; 50: The Natural History Museum, London; 51: AKG London/Cameraphoto; 53: The Art Archive/Amblin/Universal; 54: Fortean Picture Library/Tony Healy br; 54-55: Corbis/Bruce Burkhardt; 55: Corbis/George Lepp r; 56: Fortean Picture Library t; 57: Fortean Picture Library/Patterson/ Gimlin/1968 Rene Dahinden cr, b; Tony Healy tl; 58: Corbis/Carl and Ann Purcell l; 60: Kobal Collection/Hammer; 61: Ronald Grant Archive tl; Science Photo Library: Matt Meadows br; 64: Ronald Grant Archive b; 64-65: Corbis/Peter M. Wilson; 66: Ronald Grant Archive; 68: AKG London bl; 69: Nature Picture Library/Doug Allan r; 70: Corbis/Andrea Jemolo l; 71: Ronald Grant Archive/Dreamworks b; 72: Werner Forman Archive/Provincial Museum, Victoria, British Columbia, Canada bl; 72-73: Corbis/James Marshall c; 74: Kobal Collection/Icon Productions c; 75: Kobal Collection/20th Century Fox/Tursi, Mario b; 76: Ronald Grant Archive l; 77: Ronald Grant Archive b; 78: Ronald Grant Archive br; 78-9: Kobal Collection/Warner Bros; 82: Science Photo Library/National Optical Astronomy Observatories background; 83: Kobal Collection/Warner Bros/Mountain, Peter tr; 84: Corbis/Bettmann t; Williamson Collection b; 85: Corbis/Adam Woolfitt; 86-7: Ronald Grant Archive; 88-89: The Natural History Museum, London; 90-91: Werner Forman Archive/Museum of Anthropology, University of British Columbia, Vancouver; 92-93: The Natural History Museum, London.

All other images © Dorling Kindersley
For further information see:
www.dkimages.com